PRAISE FOR *THE DRAM*

"Using Jim and Kaley's practical methods in *The Drama-Free Office* is life-changing, both personally and professionally. The authors bring to the table an open and authentic style coupled with great insights and strategies to resolve issues. Personally, they have been fundamental in helping me to become a better leader. Organizationally, they have been invaluable in helping to improve communications and dynamics, and have helped to reduce the drama within my firm."

—Ron Rubin, CEO, Bridgewater Wealth & Financial Management

"Many of us experience corporate environments where dysfunctional interpersonal relationships poison the atmosphere, drain energy, and make everyone unhappy. If every manager in any organization mastered the tools in *The Drama-Free Office* in order to have effective conversations and handle conflict in a constructive way, I guarantee the result would be productive teamwork, a healthier business culture, and a thriving workforce."

—Moises Eilemberg, president and CEO, Avadyne Health

"Jim Warner and Kaley Klemp are without peers when it comes to understanding the personalities that create unintentional but extremely harmful drama in every organization. *The Drama-Free Office* provides a step-by-step approach to effectively dealing with those personalities. After reading and testing their methods in my organization, I achieved stunning results!"

—Frank Buonanotte, founder, chairman emeritus, and director, The Shopping Center Group; chairman and CEO, Barrett Rand Corporation

"We have all at one time been part of an organization that was plagued with drama. Unaddressed, this cancerous behavior can kill or cause serious damage within any organizational sector. The authors, Jim and Kaley, are masters at teaching us not only how to cure office drama, but more importantly, how to avoid it. *The Drama-Free Office* is a must-read to live drama-free personally and professionally."

—Tommy Spaulding, author of the *New York Times* bestseller
It's Not Just Who You Know

"I have worked with both Jim and Kaley on several occasions with great results. They truly understand that ineffective interpersonal dynamics can drain energy and create unproductive organizations. In this book, they teach us how to create, rather than drain, energy in the office environment. *The Drama-Free Office* captures their expertise in a succinct, easy-to-read format. Their approach for managing 'difficult personalities' is spot-on, and putting their lessons to work has led to greater business productivity and a more enjoyable environment in our workplace."

—Mark Wiseman, EVP, Canada Pension Plan Investment Board

"Jim and Kaley have crisply captured the personalities that siphon energy and productivity out of the workplace. *The Drama-Free Office* offers truly effective tools for guiding teams to perform at a very high level."

—Kent McClelland, CEO, Shamrock Foods

"*The Drama-Free Office* does exactly as promised: it offers refreshing, no-nonsense strategies to combat energy-draining office dramas. Jim and Kaley's approach will douse the drama fire in any organization."

—Rob Follows, founding partner, STS Capital Partners;
climber of Mt. Everest and the Seven Summits

"Jim Warner is the ultimate pragmatist, a relentless observer of costly conflicts and dysfunctional dramas in thousands of leadership encounters. Kaley and Jim have written a real value-added book that I intend to use to enhance my own relationships."

—Bob Buford, founder, Leadership Network; chairman, The Drucker Institute; and author, *Halftime*

"Grab your highlighter and notepad. This book is packed with useful tools for building effective and healthy relations at work . . . and at home! As a senior marketing director responsible for a variety of functions in a heavily matrixed organization, I know firsthand how important it is to be able to manage personalities in the workplace. *The Drama-Free Office* is loaded with information on what to look for in your colleagues' behavior that will help you understand, engage, and collaborate effectively with everyone on your team. From your boss to your peers and direct reports, you'll appreciate how taking responsibility for your own opinions and behaviors will encourage your business partners to follow your lead. Expect dramatic results as you get more and more comfortable using these tools."

—Bruce Smith, senior director, Marketing Operations & Communications, People to People Ambassador Programs

THE
DRAMA-
FREE
OFFICE

THE
DRAMA-

FREE
OFFICE

A Guide to Healthy Collaboration with
Your Team, Coworkers, and Boss

JIM WARNER AND KALEY KLEMP

For more information, please contact Jim Warner and Kaley Klemp at +1 303-449-7770 or www.DramaFreeOffice.com.

Published by OnCourse Publishing
Boulder, Colorado – USA
www.oncourseinternational.com

For ordering information or special discounts for bulk purchases, please contact OnCourse Publishing at +1 303-449-7770 or www.DramaFreeOffice.com.

Design and composition by Greenleaf Book Group LLC and Bumpy Design
Cover design by Greenleaf Book Group LLC and Kayla Morelli

"Autobiography in Five Short Chapters" by Portia Nelson. Copyright © 2003, from the book There's a Hole in My Sidewalk by Portia Nelson. Reprinted with the permission of Beyond Words Publishing, Inc., Hillsboro, Oregon. All rights reserved.

Publisher's Cataloging-In-Publication Data
Warner, Jim, 1950-
  The drama-free office : a guide to healthy collaboration with your team, coworkers, and boss / Jim Warner and Kaley Klemp. — 2nd ed.
   205 p. : ill ; 22 cm.
   ISBN: 978-0615659954
   1. Problem employees. 2. Interpersonal communication. 3. Teams in the workplace. 4. Leadership. I. Klemp, Kaley, 1979- II. Title.
HF5549.5.E42 W27 2011
658.3045   2011920624

Printed in the United States of America

Second Edition

First edition published in 2011 by Greenleaf Book Group, Austin TX

CONTENTS

List of Tables and Exhibits

SETTING THE STAGE

You're the head of marketing, and you've been charged with maintaining a consistent image in everything you produce. Janine is a brilliant designer and a "free spirit." Her deliverables would easily win awards for innovation but are rarely what you asked for. Enthusiastic and loyal, she responds to your verbal work assignments with, "You bet!" "I got it!" "This will be fun!" or "I can't wait to get started." But then her delivery dates slip, the quality is compromised, and the corporate image suffers. What do you do?

Lawrence is the most successful deal guy in the company. He's always pushing the envelope and, most times, it works out great. But in the Investment Committee meetings he's cynical and closed. With his quick mind and slashing tongue, he shreds others' ideas at the "what if" stage. You'd love to tap his experience as you brainstorm next year's strategic plan, but in meetings he usually remains aloof or throws out one-liners that have the other VPs either scratching their heads or scrambling for a retort. You can feel the energy drain out of the meetings he attends, and you're stumped on what to do.

Suzanne loves the responsibility and precision required in her role as corporate counsel. Her job is to keep the company safe, and she takes it very seriously. Perhaps too seriously—she combs through every contract multiple times and sends it back to the Sales team for renegotiation any time there is a hint of ambiguity or risk to the company. Meanwhile, the Sales team is going crazy. The team is obligated to revisit already-closed deals rather than building its sales pipeline. According to Suzanne, she needs to be a tough gatekeeper; otherwise the Sales team would sell the company down the river. The team members refer to her as "Dr. No" and look for any way they can to get around her. Again, you're unsure of your next steps.

You work for a workaholic, yet gifted, company founder. He's a never-ending waterfall of ideas. When he starts rambling, you're not sure whether he's giving assignments, making requests, or simply thinking out loud. If you start to ask clarifying questions, he either rolls his eyes with an "I can't believe you don't get it" message or moves on to another topic. You find yourself barely keeping up in conversations with him and in executing your assignments. You're starting to burn out. He's a brilliant strategist, the company is growing rapidly, and your options—which vest in three years—will be worth a lot, but you feel torn. Do you live with the situation, confront him, or quit?

You're totally stretched in your job—you're working seventy-hour weeks and haven't taken more than a three-day weekend in two years. It's gotten so bad your kids are calling you "Uncle Daddy." But at work, the staff loves you for coordinating events, handling details, and plugging holes. Part of you wants to blame the company, but you know you are doing it to yourself. Every time a new opportunity emerges, you want to be on the project team or event committee. You can't help yourself. But a few weeks, or even days, into these new endeavors, you start kicking yourself, asking, "Why do I keep doing this to myself?"

Why We Wrote This Book

Over the past decade, we've seen the dynamics described in the previous scenarios in hundreds of business environments. We have worked to address them with thousands of leaders, professionals, and senior associates in corporate environments, at executive team retreats, and in intimate small-group settings. We have served a vast spectrum of enterprises, from multinational public companies, to boutique entrepreneurships, to multigenerational family businesses, to professional partnerships.

At a basic level, we have found that these dysfunctional dynamics derive from *drama* in the office. This drama is the cause of the infighting, water cooler talk, meaningless meetings, and turf wars that drain energy or deflect the work team from the collaborative pursuit of goals. We've discovered that regardless of the type of organization, leaders often avoid dealing with drama in the workplace altogether, or deal with it badly.

Why do leaders settle for drama? There are two reasons: (1) They lack the skills to address difficult interpersonal topics and (2) they're fearful that confrontation will make matters worse. A volatile, yet supposedly indispensible, person will leave. A fragile person will have a meltdown. Employee morale will plummet—and it will be their fault. They'll be vilified. They'll get fired. So nothing happens.

Most of these leaders have a bookshelf of "How to build a great team" leadership books. Yet they find the one-size-fits-all techniques in most of these books don't address the nuances and underlying emotions that are usually the root cause of the problems.

When drama remains unaddressed, eventually the A-players in the company, the people you want "on the bus," will either join the dysfunction or leave. Workflow becomes so inefficient that productivity and loyalty are measured by work hours rather than accomplishments or creative breakthroughs. Managers struggle with personnel issues rather than leading a synergistic team. They spend more time addressing their own fears and doing damage control than leading out-of-the-box brainstorming sessions and bringing in new business.

It doesn't have to be this way. Once you diagnose the drama disease, you can manage it and often cure it. But you must have the courage to identify the problem and apply the appropriate management techniques. While risks exist, the prepared manager can reduce them and make major strides in reducing or eliminating drama.

In this book, we provide you with a proven set of indispensible diagnostic and management tools. You'll learn how to assess the *risks* of having the crucial encounter (nothing happens, resistance increases, chaos erupts, or the relationship ends). Once you know the risks, you can make an *informed decision* on whether to (1) invest in change, (2) cope with the situation (i.e., tolerate the behaviors of an energy-draining associate), or (3) end the relationship (i.e., the problematic individual leaves or you leave).

We'll help you identify each drama role, provide proven tools for defusing drama, and explain which ones to use with specific dramatic types. You'll also learn how to build rapport before initiating a direct conversation—whether clearing an issue, discussing performance, or undertaking any number of challenging discussions. Then, we'll teach you how to navigate the encounter. You'll learn when forceful directness is the best approach and when you are better served being delicate. Perhaps most important, you'll learn how to be grounded in yourself so you can be an agent for authenticity without becoming caught in others' dramatic behaviors.

Why You Need This Book

The individuals we work with understand that drama-prone associates sap energy from the organization. They want to plug these energy drains. They want to be in more effective relationships at all levels: subordinate, peer, and superior. They want to have the skills and courage to initiate difficult conversations. They want to guide enthusiastic, but less mature, associates. They want to tap their peers' brilliance without either frustrating themselves or stifling less-than-stellar associates. They want to drink from the spigot of a free-flowing entrepreneur without drowning in his idea flood.

You need this book if you are wasting time on drama-filled relationships and want that time back for more productive projects. If the drama runs deep in your organization, you might have fallen into complaining and cynicism yourself. Perhaps you're saying to yourself, "Okay, I get the concepts and tools, but my associates will never change. Maybe it worked in other companies, but it will never work in mine." If you take this position, you can be sure it will be self-fulfilling. You get to be the victim and rationalize your suffering. You get to be right—because nothing will change. As you read this, it might sound silly. Yet, this retreat to victimhood is rampant in most organizations.

Alternatively, you can take healthy responsibility for the situation and commit to open, curious, collaborative, and authentic interactions. If you take this courageous first step, whatever your title, others will follow your lead. It must start with you.

You want an effective, fun work environment where you face issues and address problems cleanly, and where you collaborate on solutions and celebrate successes. You want to look others in the eye without feeling fear in your chest, anger in your shoulders, or disgust in your gut. You want to plug both the psychic and financial energy drains caused by drama-riddled interactions. You're tired of the dysfunction and you're committed to authentic relationships in every part of your organization.

You are committed to your own growth and becoming a better leader, manager, or partner. You want to be drama-free. We will show you how to do all of these things.

The diagnostics and drama-shifting tools we present in the following chapters apply to groups in any size organization, in for-profits, not-for-profits, and in government. These groups include the senior executive team, a project team, a committee, the board of directors, and any one-on-one, superior-subordinate relationship. The assessments and tools can be used in managing down, across, or up in the organization. Yes, *up*—we'll even show you how to manage your boss.

Our Unique Approach

Our "lab work" for this book has included intense, candid sessions with over three thousand senior leaders in executive teams, partnerships, family businesses, elite sports teams, and other environments where drama has hampered the effectiveness of the group. In hundreds of off-site retreats, mediations, and coaching sessions, we've seen the full spectrum of drama, including whiners, pouters, kiss-ups, bullies, mavericks, narcissists, manipulators, loners, and martyrs.

We've determined that almost all of these drama-laden personas can be distilled down to the antics of four sabotaging roles: the Complainer, the Cynic, the Controller, and the Caretaker. Diagnosing and directly managing these four roles when they show up in your subordinates, your peers, your boss, and, most important, yourself, is the gateway out of drama.

CHARACTERISTICS OF THE FOUR DRAMATIC EMPLOYEE TYPES	
Drama Role	**Common Behaviors**
Complainer	Whining, waffling, resignation
Cynic	Discounting, sniping, withdrawing
Controller	Steamrolling, micromanaging, impatience
Caretaker	Overcommitment, conflict avoidance, rescuing

Many business books offer practical principles for creating trust, getting buy-in, and monitoring results. While we endorse these practices, they are usually ineffective or even damaging if the underlying drama remains unaddressed. Before you can use the tools, you must first diagnose the type of drama. Then, you must assess the person's capacity to become a productive team member. Using a medical metaphor, imagine your team members are sick. Your job is to accurately diagnose their illness, and then determine the likelihood that the illness can be managed or cured.

This means assessing areas such as your team members' ability to navigate change; their capacity to receive feedback; their track record in meeting deadlines; their willingness to delegate and empower; their actions when "bad things happen"; their maturity and effectiveness in team settings; and their overall presence around others. Based on this "diagnosis," you can then, *and only then*, determine the approaches that will optimize their capacity to collaborate with you and with the rest of the organization.

The Three Key Skills

Our goal in this book is to help you master the following three skills, which are crucial for defusing drama and enhancing authenticity in workplace relationships.

1. CATCH YOUR OWN DRIFTS INTO DRAMA

It's easy to blame interaction problems on others. After all, you're the good guy in these dynamics; why don't *they* get it? One of the most difficult challenges for aspiring leaders is to "own their stuff"—to acknowledge that they are equally responsible for relationship shortcomings. So, before you can guide others, you must take inventory of both your interaction strengths and the ways you sabotage relationships. The strength inventory is usually easy; the sabotage inventory is more difficult. It requires the vulnerability and courage to seek others' candid observations and advice about your behavior. You can't see your own blind spots, so invite your work colleagues, family members, and friends to give you timely, direct feedback. Ask them to tell you when you slip into any of the Complainer, Cynic, Controller, or Caretaker behaviors. Part III of this book shows you how to identify and get out of your own drama traps.

2. IDENTIFY THE DRAMA STYLE OF THE OTHER PERSON

Before using behavior-specific tools to create a drama-free workplace, you must understand the other person's capacity for authentic interaction. Just as you wouldn't do a tracheotomy to cure a sore throat, it's inappropriate to use ultimatums when a loyal associate makes a rare mistake. On the other hand, you don't use aspirin to treat pneumonia; neither should you coddle the judgmental bully. Skilled management calls for you to know what you're working with before you choose from your suite of interaction tools. In part II, we'll help you diagnose the specific forms of drama being acted out by your associates.

3. GUIDE OTHERS OUT OF DRAMA

Once you have diagnosed your own and others' drama tendencies, you need to choose the appropriate interaction tools to optimize the relationship. The problem with many interpersonal dynamics books is that they often assume "one size fits all" when dealing with dysfunction. Recalling the aspirin-pneumonia metaphor, certain tools, like brainstorming, won't work with Cynics or Controllers. Similarly, ultimatums cripple relationships with more thoughtful Caretakers. Part IV offers key tools for coaching others who are stuck in drama.

A Quick Tour of the Book

Part I, "Overture" (chapters 1 and 2), introduces you to the Riva Corporation, its founder-president, and a SWAT team assembled to solve a customer service crisis. In chapter 1, you'll meet Laura, the SWAT team leader, and observe her first meeting with her drama-prone team members. The remaining chapters interweave Laura's navigation of the Riva drama with stories from our consulting work with management teams. Chapter 2 provides a snapshot of the four drama types and the counterbalancing behaviors and attitudes that you must adopt to breed authenticity in any workgroup setting.

Part II, "The Four Drama Roles" (chapters 3 through 6), describes in detail the four primary drama roles: the Complainer, the Cynic, the Controller, and the Caretaker. These chapters offer insights on what's going on inside each role (i.e., why such individuals act in a dramatic fashion), the common dramatic behaviors of each role, and how to manage each role.

Part III, "Getting Yourself Out of Drama" (chapters 7 and 8), invites you to examine yourself and determine where you are prone to falling into drama. You'll learn a step-by-step process for exiting your own drama and becoming curious and open with others, no matter which drama roles they might be in.

Part IV, "Guiding Others Out of Drama" (chapters 9 through 13), presents proven tools for defusing drama and collaborating with your drama-prone associates. We'll then walk you through a proven, seven-step process to set the stage for confronting a drama-prone associate—whether a subordinate, peer, or superior—and having the drama-shifting meeting.

Finally, we will return to the drama-laden crisis at Riva Corporation and see how Laura coaches each of her drama-prone team members. We'll also show how she gets what she wants from her Controller-Caretaker boss and finds balance and authenticity in her position at Riva.

Onward!

Let the following chapters guide you in your professional growth. As you read the descriptions of the different drama types, resist the urge to indict others, and instead consider how *you* fall into drama. Choose to eliminate the drama from yourself, and then be the catalyst for others to do the same. You'll find that authenticity trumps drama every time. Your work environment—and your life—will be more productive, efficient, and fun.

PART I

Overture

In our Riva Corporation case study, Laura, the leader of a SWAT team charged to keep Riva Corporation's best client, has to manage both her edgy boss and her four drama-prone team members. As you review the drama at Riva, consider the dysfunctional associates in your organization—your peers, subordinates, and perhaps even your boss—who drain energy and inhibit collaboration and productivity. How do you tend to fuel the dysfunction by falling into your own drama patterns? What behaviors do you want from your associates? What's at risk if you approach them about the impact of their behavior on you and your colleagues?

CHAPTER 1

THE DRAMA AT RIVA

Laura took one look at her colleagues sitting around the conference table and knew she had a tough meeting ahead of her. Clearly, no one wanted to be there. And who could blame them? Riva Corporation had a crisis on its hands: The company's cornerstone client for the past decade, Highline Enterprises, was threatening to take its business elsewhere. Cliff, Riva's CEO, had formed this cross-functional SWAT team, with Laura as the lead, and ordered the group to "fix it—now!" No wonder all four managers looked like they'd just heard they were getting audited by the IRS.

Highline's president, Peter, had been a college buddy of Cliff's, and their relationship migrated to supplier-customer when Cliff launched his business services company. It was a risk that paid off for both of them: Cliff got a foothold in the industry, and his friend got a sweetheart deal on customized software and outsourced services. For several years, both firms flourished.

But as Riva Corporation boomed, Cliff focused more on growth and less on product development, customer service, internal systems, and financial management. Charismatic, gregarious, and ambitious, he had little time for the finer points of operating checks and balances, organizational development, or interpersonal dynamics. And now, a combination of screw-ups could destroy both his long-term friendship and a crucial source of revenue. Cliff's push for growth over the past eighteen months, with accelerated product development and quality assurance shortcuts, was coming back to haunt the company in a seriously flawed new product release.

Peter's frustration was justified. His friend's customized software had become an integral part of Highline's operations. Sam, Riva's VP of Sales, had guaranteed Peter enhanced functionality, increased performance, and total repair of the bugs from the previous software release. So when the new version turned out to be "less than robust," as Peter politely described it, he expected quick action from Cliff's people.

That was four months ago, and very little had changed. Fortunately, since Peter and Cliff had a lot of history with each other, Peter chose to call Cliff directly rather than simply pull the plug on the relationship.

"You guys promised me all kinds of improvements—and what we got was a raft of new bugs and a slower system," said Peter. "I'm used to working with your team to sort out new releases, but this time your Customer Service people appear to be on a permanent vacation. All we've gotten is empty promises and a litany of excuses or finger-pointing. And then you send us an invoice with a 20 percent bump in maintenance fees?"

"Peter, look, I—we—" Cliff stammered.

"Cliff, you helped me when I was just starting Highline, so I feel I owe you one more chance to make this right. However, I need to see some tangible changes soon, or I'll have to go out to bid. It's not my first choice, but several of your competitors have approached me over the past year with early-stage—and pretty attractive—proposals for switching suppliers. So far, I've politely defended our choice to go with Riva. But my patience is running out. I'll give you two weeks."

"We'll make it right, Peter. You've got my word."

They hung up—and then panic set in. Cliff was way out of his comfort zone and needed help in a hurry. He started pulling together a team to handle the disaster. As he mentally scanned his company for someone to take the lead, he locked in on one person who had the guts, experience, and skills to pull it off: Laura. He raced to her office, blurted out the problem, and then told her, "I want you to work with Sam, Theresa, Foster, and Candace on this. Set up a meeting with them immediately."

A little dazed, but grasping the importance of the project, she agreed.

"Laura, I need a workable plan on my desk by Friday. I'm counting on you to clean up this mess—you have two weeks."

The SWAT Team

Trained as a software engineer, Laura knew both the adrenalin rush and dark side of software development and project management. She joined Riva in its second year, working first as a Sales support technician and then as a Customer Service manager before being promoted to director of Operations after only three years with the firm. With her cross-department experience and dotted-line relationship with Cliff, Laura was the natural choice to lead the team for the Highline project.

Sam had hired on with Laura, but he had remained in Sales and was now managing the company's larger accounts, like Highline. He was a gifted networker, kept extensive files on his clients' situations, belonged to several prominent clubs, and relished the entertainment side of his job. As a result, many of Sam's customers socialized with him outside work. He had come to count on the perks of his position to enhance these friendships.

A generalist by nature, he liked to stay out of the details, instead relying on a couple of engineers to handle the technical questions and post-sales support. His trademark response to clients' technical concerns was, "I absolutely agree with you. Trust me—we'll get on it immediately." He protected "his" clients, always assuring them he would do whatever it took to keep them happy.

Sam had managed the relationship with Highline for several years. The account had become a big piece of his annual projected sales target—and his own bonus—so he had eagerly gone along with the product price increase. Sam had known that Peter's people were a little grumpy about the last software release. He'd flown in his best Technical Support team twice for emergency repairs. He'd also repeatedly asked the Customer Service team to give them even more special attention, so he figured everything was being handled. When he heard that Peter was about to terminate their relationship, making a serious dent in his personal income, he felt betrayed and helpless. Sam had certainly done his best, and it clearly was not his fault.

Theresa was relatively new to project management, after nearly a decade in product development. She knew Riva's software family inside out and enjoyed the cutting-edge innovation, technical challenges, and innate elegance of the company's products. It irritated her that most of the executive team—especially the Sales force—knew so little about the richness of Riva's technology and even less about the expertise required to craft it and bring it to market.

She would reluctantly attend presales calls, biting her lip during the flash-and-glitz presentations, enduring the wine-and-dine evening galas, and finding solace in the technical exchanges with the clients' internal technical teams. Since these technicians were instrumental to the buying decision, Theresa's expertise and ability to connect with them became a vital component in the sales process.

Theresa had seen the Highline meltdown coming for some time. She'd allowed the accelerated product release dates, despite knowing they would have to face a high-pressure quarter or two as bugs surfaced—just as they had so many times in the past. She had also predicted that the Riva technical team would have to endure several all-nighters to fix the problems. *Here we go again*, she thought, when she heard she'd been appointed to the SWAT team.

Foster, the director of Finance, was relatively new to the company. He'd been recruited from a large national accounting firm with the promise of line management responsibilities and the eventual opportunity to run a business unit. For his first assignment, Cliff had wanted him to restore order to the company's fragmented financial systems and act as watchdog on cash. Relishing the role, Foster quickly cleaned out the deadwood employees in the department while personally getting into the details of every project. Intolerant of mistakes or oversights, he demanded that no one in his department make a move or decision without his approval.

Like Theresa, Foster had watched the current crisis unfold over several months and felt both frustrated and angry as he witnessed the cost overruns, product delays, and lavish spending on sales calls. A couple of times he'd hinted to Cliff that he could really increase profits if given more authority. Cliff's answer—"Not just yet. Let's wait a while and see what happens"—infuriated Foster. He was ready *now!*

Normally, he could hold his temper, but once in a while, he admittedly lost it when other managers danced around difficult issues during meetings or when his own people turned in mediocre work. There were a few times when he reduced departmental budgets or vetoed capital expenditures when the managers couldn't produce crisp rationalizations for their requests. His nickname throughout the company had become "Frugal Foster," which actually pleased him. After all, if he didn't take charge and do the right thing, no one else would. He'd done his best without overstepping Cliff, so the Highline situation was certainly not his fault.

Candace wore two hats as the manager of both Customer Service and Quality Assurance. She had the rich satisfaction of ensuring that Riva's diverse products worked as advertised and then helping customers put the products to use in real-world applications. Several groups within the company saw her as the glue that bonded the company to its customers, and she loved that role.

Since her promotion from Customer Service specialist to manager two years before, she had continued to personally troubleshoot knotty customer problems while concurrently managing her two teams. Often, when her staff members would approach her with a problem they just couldn't seem to solve, Candace would cheerfully take it on herself, both to puzzle out a technical challenge and to relieve struggling colleagues. Despite an overflowing inbox and missed deadlines, she couldn't turn them down.

Recently, she had a shining moment when Sam panicked over a

prospective customer he had been cultivating for a long time who was starting to consider a competitor. Immediately coming to the rescue, Candace took three of her senior QA specialists off their project, flew them in for a week to work with the prospect's analysts to build a prototype, and helped Sam seal the deal. Foster grumbled about the excessive cost, and she fell further behind in QA testing—aggravating Theresa—but, as always, she promised to work harder to catch up.

The First Meeting

"Let me begin by thanking everyone for dropping everything and getting here so quickly," Laura said to the four managers. "I'm sure we can all think of other ways we would rather spend a Monday morning."

Everyone murmured in agreement.

"Cliff wants a solid plan from us by the end of the week," Laura continued, "and some serious movement toward fixing the problem within two weeks. So we haven't got a lot of time. Our goal for this meeting is to brainstorm ways to address this situation. As a first approach, I thought we might—"

"Laura, this is more than a 'situation,' it's a nightmare—a meltdown!" Sam interrupted. "We've done everything we can from the Sales side to hose down Peter's people, but they're still fuming. I've made personal calls to no avail. Nothing seems to be working. We need an all-hands-on-deck, whatever-it-costs blitz from every department to fix this, or we're all sunk. If Highline goes out to bid, word will get around the industry that we've lost our edge, our customers are jumping ship, and—"

"Yes, Sam, we all know this is serious," Laura said, attempting to regain the reins of the meeting. "And our job here today is to pool our best ideas for dealing with this while—"

"Oh boy, here we go again," said Theresa. "Another Mayday call from Sales. How many times have we seen this movie? Just once I'd like to hear Sam admit that he sold something we didn't have. And Sam, when was the last time you read a product manual—or even a product spec sheet? That's assuming that you can actually read. We all know you can talk." She crossed her arms and smirked. "But whatever. I'm sure you'll all come up with some clever way to dodge this bullet. Everyone will jump through hoops for a couple of weeks to bail out Sam and cover up for our lukewarm product testing. And then in a few months, we'll all end up right back here again and—"

"Gee, Theresa, that seems a little unfair," Candace said, entering the fray. "I know a few bugs got by us in the last round of testing, but we can clean those up easily in two to three days—well, maybe a little more. I think if we can just stop our bickering and work together, as Laura says, we can fix this. I've worked with the High-line analysts personally and would be happy to lead the Customer Service side of this effort. Theresa, your team needs to continue working on the next-generation products, and Sam, even though many of your field technicians started in Development, they don't have the immediate contact with it that I do. So, if you'll let me, I think I can turn this around."

"Thank you, Candace," said Laura. "Your willingness to jump in is appreciated. But I found out this morning that you are currently behind on three other Quality Assurance efforts, and one of your top Customer Service people just resigned. So, while your heart seems to be in the right place, I'm concerned that you don't have the personal capacity to take the lead here. Now, I'd like to get back to this meeting's agenda—"

"Whoa, whoa, whoa, Laura," chimed in Foster, no longer able to contain himself. "With all due respect, this isn't a time for brainstorming. It's a time for action. Right after you called this morning, I began putting together the plan that will both solve the immediate Highline problem *and* lay the fiscally responsible groundwork for hitting our P&L targets, which is what we all want, right?"

"Yes, Foster, but this is—" Laura attempted to interject.

He raised his hand to silence her. "The first step—and this is the one place I agree with Sam—is to assemble a small, top-notch team of people to resolve the Highline situation. That's easy. Sam, we'll need two of your support engineers. Theresa, we need your ace developer, plus one. And Candace, probably you and two others. That should do it. Since I'm pretty insulated from this mess, I'm the best one to lead the cross-functional team. It's also important that I do it because we need to make sure costs don't run amok as they have in the past."

Laura tried again to jump in, but Foster talked over her. "Meanwhile, we'll use this crisis as the company wakeup call to *cut costs*. Remember Cliff's number-one mantra: Increase shareholder value. We need to prune out all the excess, like Theresa's weird projects and all Sales 'entertainment.' And we'll put a hold on all the open positions, like the technician in Candace's department, at least until we get our quarterly profits back in line with projections. The only exception is the accounting manager position in my department, which has been open for nine months and is a must-fill." Foster sat back in his chair and folded his hands, looking satisfied.

An awkward silence filled the room. Laura saw an opening to try again. "Okay, now that everyone has weighed in, let's—"

"Foster, are you nuts?" said Sam. "Why are you messing with my department? We get our business by relationship selling. We can't cut entertainment—you'll single-handedly bring down the company. Our customers want to know we care about them. They *expect* the golf trips and fine dining. It's part of our industry-leading image. And bottom line only grows when top line grows. So we have to fill those three open Sales positions ASAP. If you get rid of those, my whole operation could fall apart. There's no way we could hit our sales targets, more people would leave . . . who knows what else might happen?"

"Yeah, great plan, Foster," Theresa said. "The accounting guy running a complex technology turnaround. Sam's Sales team may be a little thin on technical skills, but having you run the Highline project would be like inviting the valet parking attendant to fix a Ferrari."

Foster leaned across the table. "Well, Theresa, if you came out of your techno-dungeon with all your geek developers to get your sushi and lattes more than once a month, you'd realize I have more project management expertise in my pinky than you have in—"

"Oh, please, please, *please*," said Candace. "Look, let's all just calm down. I know there's a solution here. As I said, my team and I are willing to work evenings and weekends to smooth this over. If it takes giving up some open positions, so be it. Maybe even salary freezes for a short time while we—"

"Salary freezes!" Sam, Foster, and Theresa all yelled at once.

Laura stood up. "That's enough!" she announced.

After some grumbling, the room became quiet.

"We're done," Laura said. "We'll reconvene tomorrow morning at eight a.m. sharp. Please clear your calendars for the morning. Before then, I'll be scheduling time with each of you, one-on-one, to sort through what happened today so we can meet tomorrow in a spirit of openness, curiosity, and collaboration. Sam, I'll see you here at noon; Theresa—two o'clock; Foster—four o'clock; and Candace, since you usually stay late, I'll see you at six. Meeting adjourned."

While the participants' titles and the difficult issue may be different, most of us have likely seen—or been a part of—a similar dynamic in our own organizations: a group of well-educated, well-compensated supposed professionals deteriorating into squabbling children caught in the grip of their own self-serving views and desire to be right.

We've found that almost all team dysfunction in any company can be distilled down to four sabotaging roles: the Complainer, the Cynic, the Controller, and the Caretaker. Often, as we saw with the Highline project, these saboteurs band together to create toxic tension within the group and hijack cooperation and productivity.

But we've also found that it doesn't have to be that way. In the pages ahead, you will learn about the antidotes to drama that we've developed after working with hundreds of management teams. You will discover not only how to shift out of these behaviors yourself, but also how to coach others into a mature place of curiosity and responsibility. You'll learn the tools for helping work associates set aside their sabotaging roles of victimhood, sarcasm, control, and caretaking. You will then be able to enjoy collaborative, productive exchanges and a much more rewarding work experience.

CHAPTER 2

OVERCOMING DRAMA WITH AUTHENTICITY

During the first SWAT meeting at Riva Corporation, we saw how Laura chose to adjourn the meeting because Sam, Theresa, Foster, and Candace were not communicating in a mature, open-minded way. Instead, they had fallen into their respective sabotaging roles: the Complainer, the Cynic, the Controller, and the Caretaker.

The Four Saboteurs

Each role has its own honorable intent for getting the job done— and its own special way of being right. A *Complainer*, like Sam, would love to have a happy ending to every problem, but believes he's powerless to alter the situation. He is at the mercy of other people and situations; they have all the control. Because he's in the power of others, the Complainer feels he is "right" in his suffering and deserves to be taken care of.

Outwardly, a *Cynic*, like Theresa, claims she would love to "have it all work out," but inwardly, she doubts that it will. Even though she might not have the answer, she's certain that everyone else's ideas are wrong, and her job is to point this out. Others are shortsighted, selfish, and ignorant, and she feels she's "right" to draw attention to their flaws. She also sees the shortcomings of the potential solutions. By pointing out all the ways current ideas fall short, maybe then they'll "get it" and actually fix the problem. The Cynic doesn't really want control, but she has disdain for whoever has it.

A *Controller*, like Foster, wants work to be done efficiently and thoroughly. He knows he has the best solutions and wants it done his way—the "right" way. Give him the ball, and he'll score. But he has to have the ball. He finds others to blame for problems, since the problems wouldn't exist if he had all the power. The Controller hates both the weakness of the Complainer and the criticism of the Cynic.

Finally, a *Caretaker*, like Candace, sincerely wants to reach a positive outcome while protecting and supporting all parties. She provides temporary relief for problems—but only temporary, since new problems seem to crop up as quickly as old ones are addressed. Her approach is clearly "right," since it is most concerned with avoiding pain or discomfort and ensuring people get along with one another.

In the Riva case study, we focus on only one drama tendency in each of the four team members. In most work settings, individuals are prone to fall into varying blends of all four. Part II provides expanded definitions of the four types and explains how they show up in combinations. For example, the Complainer-Caretaker hybrid is the Martyr, and the Cynic-Controller is the Cunning Dictator.

Workplace dramas range in intensity. They may be short and

mild, or long and drawn out with many characters and "scenes." Many performances take place in a quick moment—like when Candace blurted out her comment on salary freezes—with after-effects lasting days, months, or even years. Whatever their form, all drama creators stifle enthusiasm, creativity, and progress.

The Saboteur in You

As you read the descriptions of these saboteurs—these drama kings and queens—in the following chapters, you will no doubt see their negative characteristics in your colleagues. It's easy to fall into the trap of "Aha! Now I understand why my boss is such a Controller," or "Yup, you nailed John—the team Cynic." However, it's harder to see and own these roles in yourself.

Yet, this is exactly what you must do before you can move into mature leadership.

You must become aware of the Complainer part of you, which loves to whine, feel helpless, and place blame. See your Cynic side, which likes to diminish and judge others and say, "I told you so." Notice your own Controller part, which wants to dominate people and take the reins. And, finally, acknowledge the Caretaker part of you, which wishes to make everyone feel good and play nice, even if you must do it all yourself. Only by acknowledging these parts can you make the shift to authenticity. After all, you can't solve a problem you don't think you have.

If we don't acknowledge our drama roles, we run the risk of falling into them by mistake, just as we might fall into a hole in the sidewalk. One of our favorite poems, "Autobiography in Five Short Chapters" from the book *There's a Hole in My Sidewalk*, best describes this common, unconscious error.

AUTOBIOGRAPHY IN FIVE SHORT CHAPTERS
Portia Nelson

CHAPTER ONE

I walk down the street.
There is a deep hole in the sidewalk.
I fall in.
I am lost . . . I am helpless.
It isn't my fault.
It takes forever to find a way out.

CHAPTER TWO

I walk down the same street.
There is a deep hole in the sidewalk.
I pretend I don't see it.
I fall in again.
I can't believe I am in this same place.
But, it isn't my fault.
It still takes a long time to get out.

CHAPTER THREE

I walk down the same street.
There is a deep hole in the sidewalk.
I *see* it is there.
I still fall in . . . it's a habit . . . but,
my eyes are open.
I know where I am.
It is *my* fault.
I get out immediately.

CHAPTER FOUR

I walk down the same street.

There is a deep hole in the sidewalk.

I walk around it.

CHAPTER FIVE

I walk down another street.

During stressful interactions, many of us fall into negative behaviors, or "holes in the sidewalk," that sabotage productive, efficient, and authentic collaboration. We are blind to these holes because we have been taught throughout our lives that it is more important to be right than to be authentic. Our educational system, our upbringing, and ad campaigns have stressed the importance of being right: wearing the right clothes, having the right friends, attending the right schools, and knowing the right answers. Ambiguity and wrong answers are dismissed as weaknesses. As a result, just the idea of taking healthy responsibility for every situation, especially the difficult ones we might not immediately know how to address, can make us feel both scared and vulnerable. It's much easier to defend our "right" view of the world. Although it's supposed to keep us safe, this common blind spot drastically reduces our capacity for learning and growth.

In order to get beyond "right" behavior and deal with the drama that negatively affects ourselves and our workplaces, we must open ourselves to authenticity.

The Definition of Authenticity

We define *drama* as interactions that drain energy or deflect the team from the vibrant and shared pursuit of goals. *Authenticity* is difficult to distill into an all-encompassing, one-sentence definition. Instead, we divide relationship authenticity into two components: *hard* authenticity, which we'll call *effectiveness*, and *soft* authenticity, or *awareness*.

Effectiveness is about productivity—getting things done. Addressing tasks with vigor and focus, without getting derailed by drama. Collaborating to solve difficult problems without negative judgments or skepticism. Brainstorming new opportunities—taking the go-forward windshield view—without being dragged back into prior failures or focusing on the "woulda, shoulda, coulda" rearview mirror.

Awareness is less measurable—more a sense than a metric. It includes transparency, vulnerability, maturity, presence, empathy, and consciousness. More practically, it means modeling these values while guiding others to an environment of curiosity, collaboration, and appreciation. For example, when conflict exists, put yourself in the other person's shoes and see how their logic makes sense to *them*, regardless of what *you* think. It also means honoring and mirroring back others' feelings without needing to agree with them or feeling compelled to "fix" them. Awareness is the overarching ability to interact with integrity and listen with empathy.

While many universities and executive-development courses teach effectiveness, awareness is rarely taught in business schools. But make no mistake, the impact of these softer components in virtually every life interaction determines your potential for both effectiveness and fun. Without the "soft stuff," you are likely stunting your potential for meaningful, productive relationships.

Authentic professionals are committed to lifelong learning and growth. They are open to exploring their shortcomings as managers and leaders and continually wish to improve their "game." They desire to move from being an authoritarian controller to being an inspiring delegator; from being an accommodating role player to being a decisive pacesetter; from being an argumentative skeptic to being a pioneering visionary; from a mind-set of being a misunderstood victim to taking 100 percent responsibility for their life. If you are one of these professionals, you will see tools to make these shifts in yourself and in others in the upcoming pages.

In a few instances, you will not be able to develop an authentic relationship with a coworker. In many of these relationships, you have no explicit power (e.g., the person doesn't report to you), and yet you still regularly interact with this person. In these instances, which we call *transactional relationships*, we encourage you to manage your own energy level and authentically choose to show up in the relationship, regardless of how the other person behaves.

Authentic Behaviors

In part III, you'll learn specific tools for becoming and staying authentic, so that when you do fall into your own sabotaging behaviors, you will be able to shift out of them immediately.

In the following section, we will show you how the behaviors of the four sabotaging roles described in the beginning of this chapter (Complainer, Cynic, Controller, and Caretaker) are counterbalanced by four mature, open, and authentic behaviors. They are the antidotes for drama, both in you and in others. Just as the four saboteurs can show up in combinations, these four authentic behaviors combine to form a potent, inspirational leader.

AUTHENTIC BEHAVIOR 1: TAKE HEALTHY RESPONSIBILITY FOR YOUR LIFE (ANTIDOTE FOR COMPLAINING)

Instead of complaining, commit to taking 100 percent responsibility for whatever is happening in your life. No more, no less. No one is doing it to you. Instead of retreating to accusations, excuses, and rationalizations, choose to explore your own role in creating and sustaining your current situation, especially the parts you don't like. When you take responsibility, you open the door for positive change. By examining the underlying patterns that keep you stuck, you make room for new possibilities.

When you take 100 percent responsibility for your life, you can then choose to change or keep your behaviors. This is completely your choice. If you choose to change, you might further choose to be more determined, focused, and dependable. If you choose to keep a behavior, you accept it as your conscious, intentional choice. Once you're grounded in a mature, responsible approach to life, you can become a change agent for others' transformation into authenticity.

AUTHENTIC BEHAVIOR 2: PRACTICE CREATIVITY AND COLLABORATION (ANTIDOTE FOR CYNICISM)

People care more about how your wisdom, experience, and awareness can help them learn and grow than how smart you are. If you have a keen mind, rather than using it to point out flaws and things that could go wrong, engage your critical thinking and wit to come up with new ideas that haven't been explored before. In doing so, you will engender curiosity and a thirst for new knowledge in others.

Work with your colleagues to generate options, stay open to new and creative possibilities, and stretch yourself and others outside of your intellectual comfort zones. Your curiosity can lead others to new possibilities or breakthroughs. The collective group trumps the singular mind, especially when facing emotional dilemmas where there is no clear answer. And, even if your idea is the best, having buy-in from others ensures that it gets implemented. Through collaboration, you open the possibility of arriving at a better solution than you could have conceived on your own.

Defensiveness, withdrawal, and cynicism sabotage learning. Rather than closely guarding your ideas against the attacks of others, share your thinking openly, welcoming others' feedback. As you share your thoughts and emotions freely, your vulnerability, discernment, and care for others will keep the entire group engaged.

AUTHENTIC BEHAVIOR 3: EMPOWER OTHERS AND EXPRESS GRATITUDE (ANTIDOTE FOR CONTROLLING)

Rather than trying to do everything yourself—telling others what to do and how to do it—practice empowerment. Enduring leaders are committed to the growth of their people. Your drive to be the best can inspire and motivate others to follow your example. However, if it becomes a competition with them, if you only care about winning, you lose your inspirational edge. By releasing control and choosing to empower others, you invite them to step out of your shadow and into their own light. And, in the long run, a team of honored individual lights invariably outshines the singular light of the leader.

Similarly, practice gratitude. Whenever someone approaches you with feedback, set aside your tendency to rationalize your own behavior, and instead express your appreciation for their insights, regardless of the form of their delivery. Every obstacle has a lesson if you are open to it. As you become more thankful for the good things in your life, fewer events and people will rattle you, distract your focus, or drain your energy. Your associates at work will both admire you more *and* support you more if your approach is one of optimism and gratitude. Imagine how uplifting you will become toward others if you approach all situations and relationships with appreciation for both the challenges and the possibilities.

AUTHENTIC BEHAVIOR 4: BE CARING AND SET BOUNDARIES (ANTIDOTE FOR CARETAKING)

Many of our clients at first don't see caretaking as a form of drama. What could be more noble than the intention to protect and support others? The drama arises when the caretaker goes beyond supporting, to protecting, rescuing, smothering, and enabling. Caretakers take the burden of the problem squarely on their shoulders, perpetuating others' dramatic behaviors. Caring, as opposed to caretaking, is grounded in empathic listening and simply being present, without the need to cure, heal, or fix.

When another person is caught in drama, the caretaker's first reaction is either to join them or to try to rescue them. The authentic approach is to offer encouragement, advice, and coaching so the other person learns to address the situation on his or her own. This prevents dependency and instead breeds responsibility and growth in others who are still stuck in drama.

Caretakers often ignore the fuel gauge on their energy and run their tank dry. Authentic caring includes care for yourself, knowing both your capacities and your limits. Yes, it's noble and appropriate to serve and support others, as long as you treat yourself with the same care. Authentic, caring people keep adequate fuel in their energy tank by setting and enforcing clean boundaries. They then monitor and preserve their energy for its highest and best uses.

———————

In summary, when you find yourself slipping into any of the drama roles, commit to shifting into the authentic behaviors shown below.

DRAMA ROLES AND AUTHENTIC BEHAVIOR ANTIDOTES	
Drama Role	**Authentic Behavior Antidote**
Complainer	Taking healthy responsibility
Cynic	Creativity and collaboration
Controller	Empowerment and gratitude
Caretaker	Caring and boundaries
All	Curiosity and openness

Regardless of your drama tendencies, an authentic approach to relationships requires a willingness to replace your limited viewpoints with a curiosity for the views of others. You must actively take part in all interactions, from brief one-on-one exchanges to multiday strategic off-sites, with the genuine desire to learn from others, receiving their feedback—and even criticism—with open-mindedness. Attaining this level of growth calls for both self-discipline and encouragement from others as you step out of drama and adopt the four authentic behaviors as antidotes for your own drama.

PART II

The Four Drama Roles

Now that you have been exposed to the Highline crisis and the shift from drama to authenticity, we are ready to develop a much deeper understanding of the four drama roles and how you can manage them. As you read through the next four chapters, think about the relationships in your workplace and about your own drama tendencies.

CHAPTER 3

THE COMPLAINER

"Nobody knows the trouble I've seen."

Complainers excel at playing the injured party; they elevate griping to an art form. They believe that life is too hard and that everything is happening *to* them. When trouble arises, they look for a bad guy to take the fall, because nothing can possibly be their fault.

At Riva Corporation, Sam, the Sales VP, is stuck in Complainer victimhood. He struggles to focus in times of stress and refuses to accept responsibility for any problems. Regarding the Highline crisis, his "we've done everything we can" position exemplifies the Complainer. He has his own comfortable domain to manage and doesn't want any disruptions. Just give him what he wants, pay him well, and leave him alone.

When pressures mount, Complainers want someone to give them a pain-free exit rather than staying curious and looking for creative solutions. Instead of collaborating, they moan about how hard they work and how their colleagues fail to appreciate their efforts. In especially tough situations, Complainers become moody or unpredictable. Not wanting to set them off, others will walk on eggshells, trying to calm them down or gain their favor.

The Complainer Mind-Set

Underneath their whining, blaming, and rationalizations, Complainers often are filled with fear and apprehension. Because they refused to learn—or were never taught—how to face adversity, they lack coping skills and are afraid they won't be able to survive on their own. To them, the world is a scary place and, like helpless insects, they are trapped in the web of its evil spiders.

Many Complainers were never held accountable for their behavior, so they find it impossible to sit in discomfort. They'll do anything they can to avoid conflict and pain, from denying reality to relying on others to rescue them. Life is such a burden for them that they feel they deserve a free pass and expect everyone else to do the heavy lifting.

Though they'll rarely admit it, Complainers actually want clear boundaries, backed by compassionate support and guidance. Since they see the world as unsafe, they long for a secure environment in which they can feel safe and begin to take responsibility for their lives.

Complainer Behaviors

Like an immature teenager busted for alcohol (or virtually anything), the Complainer reacts to trouble by proclaiming innocence. After all, he didn't write the script, and he's certainly not the director; he's just a bit player in the melodrama called work. The

Complainer always "intended to do better," but just didn't have the time, money, or support. Something out of his control (e.g., access to certain data, spending authority, decision rights) was missing or wrong. His common lament: "If only . . ."

In addition to always having a ready excuse, experienced Complainers further distance themselves from responsibility by criticizing power figures (the boss or project leader is always a prime target) for too much work, lack of understanding, or hidden agendas. Claiming to be surrounded by manipulators (Cynics) and tyrants (Controllers), they share their "poor me" story with Caretakers, persuading these rescuers into taking away their pain and creating a classic victim-enabler codependency.

Because Complainers rarely solve problems proactively, they struggle to get any traction in addressing life's challenges. They pick the easier items on their to-do lists rather than attacking the hard projects or having the tough conversations. When pressed for their opinions, recommendations, or timelines, Complainers hesitate, drag their feet, or defer to others' wishes. They stay noncommittal, preferring to play it safe because commitments lead to accountability for their actions. A common tactic is some variation of "I don't know. How am I supposed to know? Just tell me what you want me to do."

Many Complainers lack discipline and show up unprepared, especially those who have rarely experienced negative consequences for their actions. They may have several projects going at once, but seldom complete any of them. Any roadblock provides an excuse for delays or the need for more resources.

Under pressure, many people legitimately have difficulty thinking clearly. Yet Complainers overreact in this situation. Sam's outburst—"It's a nightmare!"—deflects his responsibility and derails constructive suggestions. Once someone else makes the decision and sets a course of action, it's amazing how quickly most Complainers regain their crisp thinking and clear views on "what should have been decided." This provides the perfect excuse to reenter the cycle of complaining and helplessness.

Chronic Complainers are often skilled manipulators. One of their favorite tactics is trying to instill guilt in others: "Why are you doing this to me? If you *really* understood [me, the problem, the situation], you'd take care of me and give me what I want. But since you obviously don't understand, I'll just suffer while doing my duty."

COMMON COMPLAINER BEHAVIORS

1. Finding ready excuses for mistakes

2. Looking for someone or something to blame

3. Sidestepping the tough tasks and waffling when others make requests

4. Resigning to the will of others: "Tell me what you want me to do."

5. Dabbling in a number of projects and seldom finishing

6. Regularly griping about a lack of support and resources

7. Struggling with thinking clearly under pressure, quickly deferring to others

8. Placing guilt on others: "Why are you doing this to me?" "You just want to hurt me," or "You don't really care about me."

Managing Complainers

Complainers tend to be bright people. If you can coax them out of their victimhood and encourage them to take responsibility for both their current and future work life, they will often be transformed into valued colleagues. Most teenagers, when coached with a blend of boundaries and compassion, become productive adults. The same logic applies to Complainers.

THE COMPLAINER SUBORDINATE OR PEER

How should Laura approach Sam? When managing a complainer on your team, you need to strike a delicate balance between holding him accountable to specific metrics and giving him the flexibility to do things his way.

Complainers need structure to mature. With entrenched Complainers, this might mean resorting to ultimatums or performance plans. Present these clearly and calmly, and remain unaffected by their whining, guilt trips, pouting, or other theatrics. Sam needs not only a budget to entertain clients, but also a plan for generating new sales, servicing existing accounts, and handling minor crises that don't require other departments to drop everything.

Build rapport with Complainers by praising their movements toward curiosity and initiative. Avoid the temptation to overdo it out of your desire to gain their approval. Experienced Complainers will sense any need to be liked or fix problems, and will take advantage of your rescue efforts. Over time, you can shift from one-sided ultimatums to collaborative agreements, as long as the consequences for missing milestones—and the rewards for achieving them—are clear.

When providing Complainers with feedback on their actions, you can expect pushback. They don't like being forced out of their comfort zones and will probably cast you as the bad guy. They might escalate into passive-aggressive behaviors, amplify drama in their work group, and become less reliable in their interactions. They might complain to your boss or even threaten to leave.

Don't buy into any of it. If it results in an argument, you lose. If you cover for them, they won't confront their problematic habits. Remember that this is just part of the act they've honed for many years. It's not about you. Relax, take a deep breath, and stay clear, compassionate—and firm. Anticipate their antics and be prepared to calmly and explicitly state consequences. Your job is to manage their behavior until, hopefully, they reach a place of maturity, with the potential for collaboration.

TIPS FOR COACHING COMPLAINER SUBORDINATES OR PEERS

1. Offer sincere, specific compliments when they perform well, and tell them you value their contributions.

2. Focus on the facts and avoid any judgments they could take personally. Provide concise justification for any recommended actions, but avoid long rationalizations.

3. Give them space to consider your feedback—but not too much. Set specific times for follow-up.

4. If they seem overwhelmed, offer reassurance about your confidence in them and their ability to stretch, but resist rescuing them.

5. Offer a range of choices acceptable to you and let them decide their own course of action.

6. Make clear agreements and always keep your end. Establish and enforce explicit consequences for broken commitments.

7. Acknowledge their capabilities and remind them of their responsibilities.

THE COMPLAINER BOSS

Most Complainer supervisors like attention. They also need to like you before they'll welcome what you have to say. When you do have their ear, praise their mature behaviors, such as supporting *their* boss, completing a key project on time and on budget, brainstorming solutions, or effectively managing risk. Tell others about these behaviors—with your boss present—so she begins to associate them with authentic leadership.

Complainer bosses are often indecisive, so make sure you don't become the scapegoat for their inability to establish metrics or boundaries. Gently, but firmly, demand clear and measurable agreements with them about your own projects, and remember to compliment them when they do make decisions.

Since Complainers often want to dump their problems on others, avoid becoming your supervisor's confidant. If she likes you or sees you as an ally, she might confide in you about others in the organization, placing you in the center of drama. This can lead to a sticky, even dangerous codependence: If you later try to detangle yourself from this unhealthy relationship, you run the risk of being abandoned—or perhaps fired—by your boss. If you do find yourself in an awkward, confidential conversation, you might say something like, "I'm uncomfortable with where this conversation about [another person or any uncomfortable topic] is going. I appreciate your candor with me, but I think it would be better if I weren't involved."

TIPS FOR COACHING COMPLAINER BOSSES

1. Relate to them with a positive attitude and express an interest in their ideas.

2. Give them lots of personal attention. Regularly appreciate them or their accomplishments and acknowledge their mature behaviors, especially decisiveness.

3. Show your support for them, particularly during challenging times. Let them know you have their back.

4. Whenever you present a problem to them, come prepared with your recommended solutions. Offer to take responsibility for implementing them.

5. Always stay calm and nonjudgmental. Avoid being drawn into gossip or pity parties, or becoming their confidant.

6. Put yourself in your boss's shoes. Anticipate the issues your boss is facing with *his* boss or board. Connect your reasoning to the bigger picture.

CHAPTER 4

THE CYNIC

"That will never work."

Intelligent and creative individualists, Cynics can both understand and manage complex situations. Yet, rather than using their intellectual and communication gifts in a collaborative, uplifting manner, they wield them as weapons to drive home their point or shred the arguments of others.

Cynics are right, and that's all you need to know. They view others' feedback as jealous or judgmental attempts to undermine their efforts and attack their position. According to them, all discussions and brainstorming sessions are either a waste of time or devious tactics meant to defeat them. As a result, Cynics are always on guard and feel compelled to defend their turf, first by explaining and then by rationalizing. If they can't get the upper hand that way, they simply retreat to their castle of rightness and pull up the drawbridge.

With a razor sharp mind and tongue, Theresa, the head of Development, likes to live in her own little world of expertise at Riva Corporation and fume at the ineptness of the other department managers. When the Highline crisis arose, she directed her blaming, "here we go again" comments toward her associates. Although a pro at predicting problems, she presents few, if any, constructive solutions.

During such stressful times, the Complainer will express helplessness ("It's out of my control. There's nothing I can do."), whereas the Cynic will express hopelessness ("There's nothing anyone can do. Why bother?"). Then, when someone offers a possible remedy, Cynics are quick to shoot it down: "It will never work." They insist they're acting as watchdogs for the organization, keeping it from running amok. In reality, their resignation sucks the energy out of a room. Colleagues become reluctant to share ideas, knowing that the pessimistic Cynic is ever ready to tear them down—and innovation suffers.

The Cynic Mind-Set

Take away a Cynic's bravado and self-righteousness and you'll often discover a needy, vulnerable person who is afraid he's not good enough. To compensate for their lack of self-confidence, Cynics will go to great lengths to prove they are smarter—and better—than others. Accordingly, they hold contempt for less-competent people, especially those who dare to confront them.

Like Complainers, Cynics seldom take responsibility for their circumstances, refusing to admit to their own shortcomings. They believe problems arise from the foolishness of others, so they approach any difficulty with judgment, impatience, and blame.

Many Cynics hunger to be perceived as gifted models of integrity.

They want work to be done carefully and correctly. Driven by the need to be right, they detest ambiguity or uncertainty and attempt to figure out life instead of just living it. Most yearn for recognition as masters in their fields and have strong ideals they want to have valued by others. They long to hear others tell them, "Wow, that's a really good idea!"

Cynic Behaviors

The Cynic often disrupts meetings with sarcastic one-liners, derailing the discussion just when ideas begin to flow. He takes a passive approach, appearing to defer or disengage—only until his own motivations, logic, or beliefs are challenged. At that point, he can quickly become agitated and aggressive, and might launch an attack.

Cynics prefer debate to resolution. Like many political pundits, talk radio personalities, and editorial columnists, they enjoy being witty and cutting, but rarely provide workable solutions. They thrive in debate because it keeps the problem "out there." Resolution means action and accountability; it's much easier to criticize from the sidelines, as Theresa did when Foster proposed cost-cutting. She questioned his competence and undermined any possibility of a collaborative exchange, without offering an alternative solution.

Some Cynics turn even casual conversations into win-lose debates, confident they can talk their way into getting what they want. They can argue whatever point serves them in the moment.

Because they know what's "right" in all circumstances, Cynics are quick to criticize and point the finger when mistakes occur, using some variation of "I told you so. You should have listened to me."

For example, Theresa reminded the Highline project team that she saw these problems months prior. Yet, when Cynics are probed for their solutions ("Okay, what would *you* do?"), they typically shrug and retreat back into passivity and hopelessness.

Often temperamental, Cynics can make any interaction an ordeal—for everyone involved. When stuck in Cynical behavior, all but the most tenacious communicators avoid face-to-face dialogue unless absolutely necessary. Some Cynics will withdraw into their work, their team, or their travel to avoid dealing with colleagues outside their domain. When required to participate in brainstorming sessions, they can seem aloof or preoccupied, as evidenced by their body language. Theresa's smirk and crossed arms at the meeting are examples.

Although not disruptive, this kind of behavior still makes collaborative associates wonder, "What's going on inside him?" When the Cynic does speak, he usually responds like a protective prince defending his province. While he might occasionally ask about others' domains, he tends to be highly private, almost secretive, about his own. Sharing it might diminish his influence or invite feedback and criticism.

A person with both Cynic and Complainer tendencies is the Ultimate Pessimist. This combines intellectual sparring with an ongoing lament about the problems everywhere. According to the Ultimate Pessimist, the situation is hopeless and he is helpless and uninterested in changing anything.

COMMON CYNIC BEHAVIORS

1. Discounting the ability of others and pointing out their flaws

2. Staying closed to the direction, feedback, or advice of others

3. Rebelling against authority by either sniping (aggressive) or withdrawing (passive)

4. Refusing to change after developing a position

5. Manipulating or outwitting others to achieve a goal

6. Relishing the role of nonconformist or devil's advocate

7. Transforming interactions into debates to avoid problem solving

8. Responding to others' ideas with doom and gloom: "It will never work."

Managing Cynics

Underneath their arrogant or detached facades, Cynics tend to possess extraordinary insight, focus, and imagination. When they can channel their talents toward a higher purpose—rather than protecting their turf or attacking others—reformed Cynics become innovative contributors. They can quickly cut to the heart of difficult issues and recognize patterns, making them both valuable collaborators and savvy risk managers.

When properly guided and appreciated, Cynics can learn to set aside their need to win and be right. They can then tap into their natural ability to explore—and inspire others to do the same.

THE CYNIC SUBORDINATE OR PEER

Because cynicism and criticism in organizations are toxic, managers need to immediately confront Cynics and condemn this behavior. It must not be tolerated. Period.

Cynics frequently look for a fight. Don't play their game. Trying to appease or negotiate with entrenched Cynics is usually futile. Instead, you need to be direct, succinct, and calm when meeting with them. Precisely and decidedly describe the behavior you want, and then use hard boundaries, clear agreements, and—if necessary—explicit ultimatums.

Cynics may resist at first and try to debate you on the fine points of your requests, looking for loopholes in your logic. Ignore their antics and stay on target. Firmly demand respectful, mature collaboration. Challenge them to figure out tough problems that "no one else has been able to crack." Perhaps finish with an appreciation of their talents and potential, even if they are dismissive.

In the worst-case scenario, if you find yourself at wit's end with a chronic Cynic or Ultimate Pessimist, remember that they fear being incompetent or vulnerable. Their off-putting behavior isn't about you or the team; it's usually about the Cynic's need to be recognized as capable. Helping a Cynic feel good about his efforts—and himself—can provide the catalyst for positive change.

If you choose to establish a performance plan for a Cynic, prepare specific, written metrics to facilitate improvement. Be ready for a battle over these, even to the point of legal involvement. The "uncloaked" Cynic might also launch a campaign against you among coworkers. If you choose to end the relationship, anticipate resentment that will test your boundaries. The rejected Cynic can be extremely unpredictable, so prepare for high drama.

TIPS FOR COACHING CYNIC SUBORDINATES OR PEERS

1. Hold your ground when reprimanding them, without being overpowering. Stay direct, truthful, fair, and explicit about your wants.

2. Focus on their energy-draining behaviors and stick to the facts. Make sure all your comments are accurate and sincere. Avoid any judgments or accusatory remarks they could take personally.

3. Dialogue about possibilities, and then ask for their recommendations. Or, offer a small number of specific choices (all okay with you), and let them choose.

4. Remember to show appreciation as much as you offer constructive criticism.

5. Be thorough when giving directives and provide a brief rationale for your decisions. Whenever possible, allow them to overrule you in some aspect of the decision so they can get a "win."

6. Let them be your teacher, and regularly ask for their ideas. Praise novel thinking.

7. Express confidence in their abilities and then challenge them to act outside their comfort zone.

8. Help them see positive outcomes instead of potential problems and dead ends.

THE CYNIC BOSS

Since a Cynic boss enjoys showing how smart he is, becoming a student to him is the best managing-up strategy; it will allow you to effectively lead him to more authentic behaviors. Express interest in his areas of expertise and ask him to teach you about them. A Cynic supervisor usually likes to talk about himself. When appropriate, let him. Find out what he likes and discuss his favorite topics. Once you've developed a good relationship with your supervisor, compliment him for trusting others, for rewarding good behavior, for collaborating, and especially for accepting others' views over his own.

Cynic bosses often breed Cynic subordinates. Your attempts to learn from him and your affirmations of his positive behaviors might be viewed as "kissing up" by your peers. So what? If others fall prey to his cynicism, it's their choice. Your objective is a more collaborative relationship with your boss and a more productive, fun work environment. Choose whatever tactics you need to make this happen, as long as they are ethical.

Since Cynic supervisors are highly sensitive to duplicity and betrayal, your best efforts may still prove ineffective. If you choose to stay, you can cope by keeping all discussions at an intellectual level, keeping the conversation out of riskier emotional terrain.

TIPS FOR COACHING CYNIC BOSSES

1. Take genuine, detail-level interest in their areas of expertise, their ideas, and their favorite topics. Let them be your teachers.

2. Appreciate them and recognize their intellect and accomplishments, but do so in private. Be specific and brief in your comments to avoid coming across as fawning.

3. Affirm them when they display trust toward you or others.

4. Thoroughly prepare for all meetings with them and come ready to support your positions. Share your thinking, including the options you dismissed and the rationale for your recommendations.

5. Actively participate when they want to debate, but let them get the final win.

6. Become an expert in your field, since Cynics like to surround themselves with other smart people.

CHAPTER 5

THE CONTROLLER

"Nobody does it better than me!"

Compelled to be the best, the Controller obsesses about winning. He believes that others are constantly seeking the same, so he must overpower them to prevail. Life is tough and only the strong survive.

The Controller is convinced that he has all the right answers, both for himself and for the organization. Consequently, it is his job to tell people what to do—and stay on them to make sure they do it—since their efforts are rarely good enough. And if something goes wrong, someone must pay—but not him.

At Riva Corporation, Foster runs the Finance department with an iron fist, insisting on making virtually every decision. He values efficiency and productivity far above interpersonal dynamics. Quick to judge, he rants during the Highline meeting about the faults of the other departments and blurts out directives, careful to ensure his area's needs are met. When the others question his ideas, he insults them, further distancing himself from his peers.

The Controller Mind-Set

Unlike Complainers, Controllers refuse to surrender to the whims of others, especially to weak authority figures. To protect themselves, they must be invincible and keep anyone else from getting the upper hand. As a result, they have great difficulty yielding responsibility to others. But when mistakes surface, Controllers, like Complainers and Cynics, deny culpability and usually have a host of scapegoats readily available.

We've seen that Cynics use cunning to achieve their goals, needing to be perceived as intellectually superior to others: "I win, you lose." On the other hand, Controllers rely on intensity and aggression to get what they want, and they need others to see them as being in charge. Their attitude: "I will win—and I don't care about anyone else."

Extreme Controllers come from a place of self-absorption or arrogance, consumed by a desire for the spotlight. And the only way they can get that attention is by holding the decisive command position. Focused solely on their own concerns and grounded in a deep sense of entitlement, they are usually oblivious to the needs of others.

Given their compulsion to do everything right—as defined by them—many Controllers believe they are serving a higher cause. They just want the job performed their way and long to be recognized and rewarded for their efforts.

Controller Behaviors

Like the Cynic, the Controller tends to be a perfectionist. Both saboteurs claim to know the right solution, but Cynics usually just talk about it without taking action. In contrast, Controllers take charge of everything while setting impossible goals for themselves, as well as for their subordinates. Often workaholics, Controllers will obsess over tasks and pick and probe relentlessly at others' efforts. They'll reward loyal subjects who toe the line, but will deliver public consequences to those who fail to meet their expectations.

Although Controllers might appear benevolent to cooperative underlings who are hungry for their approval, they will quickly attack anyone who questions their motives or methods. Some Controllers will obstruct rising stars in the organization, especially if the up-and-comers might make them look bad. To satisfy their need for power, Controllers will also ignore or rebel against superiors' directives and feedback, especially constructive criticism. Cocky and impatient, many often act rashly—recall Foster's proposal to slash costs and cancel development projects.

Some Controllers come across as mavericks—think James Bond or Rambo. Blunt, indiscreet, and self-righteous, they claim to be beacons of truth. Less-mature associates in an organization will mistake the maverick's bravado for seasoned leadership and follow him into unwinnable causes. The Controller reveals little about his thinking but insists his actions have a noble purpose, giving him an out if difficulties arise.

Foster's bold confidence lacks grounding. He isn't serving the higher cause of Riva Corporation, nor is he collaborating with his team members to create the best solution. Instead, he's certain that he has *the* way out of the trouble. His brash statement—"I have more project management expertise in my pinky than you have . . ."—both aggravates and alienates colleagues, and overstates his talents.

When Controller behaviors blend with either Cynic or Complainer traits, it creates an ugly combination. The Controller-Cynic, also known as the Cunning Dictator, crushes any resistance to his mandates and is virtually unapproachable. Most dictators of small countries fall into this category, as well as dictators of small *companies*. The smokescreen of the Cynic mixed with the power of the Controller breeds fear in associates and subordinates. Perhaps worst of all, the Cunning Dictator is usually a skilled communicator who positions himself as a benevolent change agent to the rest of the world, but acts as a condescending elitist inside the organization. Anyone foolish enough to question him becomes a primary target for termination.

Not quite as toxic, the Controller-Complainer combination, or the Weak King, often shows up in smaller organizations and family businesses. This form of saboteur lacks the Cynic's manipulation skills and fortitude. Typically, he has been given—rather than earned—responsibility and never learned how to use his power for higher goals. Thin-skinned about criticism and fearful of losing control, Weak Kings tend to revel in their own insignificant accomplishments, yet belittle others' minor mistakes. When trouble strikes, they'll immediately proclaim their innocence and either fall into the misunderstood whining of the Complainer or offload culpability to an unsuspecting subordinate. Authentic, mature coworkers easily threaten them.

COMMON CONTROLLER BEHAVIORS

1. Insisting on overseeing every decision and refusing to delegate
2. Hijacking discussions and ordering others around, even without the authority to do so
3. Setting impossible expectations
4. Placing productivity, efficiency, and action above relationships
5. Easily losing patience with indecisive people
6. Becoming angry quickly when confronted
7. Ignoring or challenging superiors' directives

Managing Controllers

Recovering Controllers can become valuable assets to an organization. They champion efficient and thorough completion of assignments and can be tough-minded and resolute under pressure. Most Controllers derive meaning, and often their identity, from their accomplishments, making them highly productive associates. They might still want to lead a domain of their own, but with guidance, they can also be loyal to authentic authority figures.

THE CONTROLLER SUBORDINATE OR PEER

To manage Controllers, supervisors must give them some area to call their own—a "sandbox" they can oversee. It doesn't have to be large, but it must be theirs. They might ask for more than they can handle or you're willing to grant. As Foster did, they might grumble when they don't get it all. They'll continue to push until you set a boundary, so be prepared to do this.

Because Controllers need to be seen as powerful, praise them for their influential presence, and then guide them toward becoming *empowering* rather than domineering. They also desperately want to lead, so coach them in the art of delegation, impressing upon them that enduring leadership and real power are based on the ability to inspire others to accomplish difficult tasks.

Since Controllers are usually motivated by recognition of accomplishments, create a visible scoreboard to track their achievements. They relish a challenge—so give one to them and push them to push themselves. Set explicit metrics, especially mutually agreed-upon, intermediate milestones for measuring progress. This is especially important with Controller-Complainers, who will gravitate toward ambiguous agreements. Give them the responsibility they crave, encourage them toward measurable achievements, and accept no excuses.

Controllers often resist short-term appraisals with some variation of "I've got it—trust me" bravado. Given their energy and aura of self-reliance, you might be tempted to relax your evaluation criteria. Don't. Instead, gently, yet firmly, acknowledge their passion, commitment, and self-confidence, but *still* demand the intermediate checks. Then, get out of their way, accepting that once you turn them loose, you'll have a difficult time revisiting and revising metrics.

With Controllers who are first-time managers, no matter how diligent you are about encouraging them to delegate and empower others, they'll likely drift back into "I'll do it myself" behaviors. Their independence and work ethic have served them a long time, and these habits die hard. When reformed Controllers slip into their old ways, remind them of the bigger goal (a high-functioning team) and their crucial role (empowerment, guidance, and delegation) in realizing it. Emphasize the importance of collaboration among their subordinates and the development of their successor.

When the situation calls for a reprimand, you must meet the Controller's challenging presence with your own confident stance. Address the issues calmly and candidly. Controllers understand boundaries and power, and will respond to clear commands or ultimatums. Make sure to finish the conversation by appreciating their gifts of tenacity and spirited toughness, along with affirming your belief that they are an able leader in their specific area.

As Controller subordinates move to a more mature place, you might notice them beginning to become more open. This is a huge stretch for them, so applaud them for it. Do the same when they display patience, hear others' perspectives, and question their own version of what's right. And when a Controller subordinate delivers successfully on a deadline or budget, commend him publicly for making big things happen.

TIPS FOR COACHING CONTROLLER SUBORDINATES OR PEERS

1. Applaud initiative and independence, while still requiring intermediate milestones.
2. Establish boundaries for their own "sandbox" and then let them run it.
3. Praise them for empowering others and for proactively informing you of their activities.
4. Reprimand swiftly, decisively, and privately. Reaffirm the explicit behaviors you expect.
5. Consider having a visible scoreboard for measuring their achievements and progress.
6. Dialogue about possibilities and then ask for recommendations. Or, offer a small number of specific choices (all okay with you), and let them decide.
7. Demand their full support once a decision is made, even if they don't agree with it. Don't allow second-guessing.

THE CONTROLLER BOSS

Overtly confronting a Controller boss is risky and can limit your career. Instead, build a relationship with him before initiating a difficult conversation. Study his behaviors, attitudes, and willingness to receive feedback.

A Controller boss expects you to perform well so that he'll look good. Focus on delivering quality work on time and on helping him earn recognition. Since a Controller expects strength and energy from himself and others, hold your ground, speak your truth, and perform assigned tasks with high integrity.

Compliment your boss for his efficiency, which he highly

values. Note, however, that Controllers are sensitive to false praise or fawning, so keep the appreciation short and specific. Deliver compliments with sincerity, and in a matter-of-fact way.

As poor delegators, Controllers will often give vague or incomplete instructions. They assume you'll know what to do and then reprimand you when your deliverable differs from their expectation. Consequently, you must clearly define goals and time frames up front. They might become irritated at your persistence or your "ignorance," but insist on explicit agreements. Better to risk their frustration early in the game than to miss deadlines or fail to meet their expectations later.

In the worst-case scenario, if you work for a Controller who resists coaching or leadership development, understand that the probability of authentic interactions is low and that your best coping strategy is to stay below his radar screen. If you're willing to take the risk, you might go over his head to seek reassignment or upper-level backing for your role. This is usually a high-stakes move, so be prepared for the Controller to react with swift, angry retaliation, which might mean your termination.

TIPS FOR COACHING CONTROLLER BOSSES

1. Make them look good so they earn external recognition.

2. Accept your role as the reliable soldier and demonstrate your support and trustworthiness, especially during challenging times. Controller bosses reward loyalty.

3. Establish unambiguous agreements about deliverables and time frames.

4. Avoid complaining or appearing insecure—they expect strength and energy from others.

5. Praise them for delegating and for displaying trust toward you or others.

6. If they micromanage you or override your best ideas, swallow your pride and let them have the last word.

CHAPTER 6

THE CARETAKER

"No, no . . . let me do that for you.
I'll take care of it."

Like most of us, a Caretaker wants to help others, feel appreciated, and live in a stable, calm environment. Unlike many of us, though, he becomes obsessed with these desires and will go to great lengths to satisfy them, including sacrificing himself.

Caretakers believe the right thing to do is get along, provide for others, and keep the peace. Consumed by others' needs and opinions, they are constantly evaluating their interactions: "How am I doing?" How is everyone else doing?" "Do they like me?" "How can I belong?"

Typically, Caretakers are highly productive associates in environments that require—and reward—long hours, no whining, and head-down work. Problems arise, however, when they take on more than they can do, or when a Caretaker moves into a leadership role.

To be effective, he must now blend empathy with accountability, but he usually overdoes compassion and balks at making tough decisions, having difficult conversations, or holding boundaries.

At Riva Corporation, Candace is very loyal and loves being a proactive problem-solver. With such admirable qualities, she might appear more noble than her peers. But on the contrary, just like the other forms of drama, her compulsive need to please and be indispensable hinders collaboration and drains energy, especially in the long run.

The Caretaker Mind-Set

Most Caretakers have had a negative experience with conflict and made the unconscious decision to avoid it at all costs. They associate it with loss or rejection, so any form of interpersonal tension—from mild annoyance to overt anger—threatens their sense of equilibrium. Although few people enjoy arguments, Caretakers either flee from them or act as peacemaker. Somewhere along the way, they determined that the best way to make it in the world is to perform well and be nice.

Most Caretakers' strongest desire is for other people to like them. Even when things seem to be going well, for a Caretaker it never feels like enough. Rather than risk losing approval, they sacrifice themselves for others.

Whereas the Controller likes to be recognized for power, the Caretaker seeks appreciation for serving. The Caretaker wants to help others *and* be recognized for it. Not as overtly demanding as the Cynic, the Caretaker craves recognition: "We couldn't have done it without you. Thanks."

A mature person can empathize with associates in need while

staying unattached from their situation or desired outcome. On the other hand, the Caretaker feels driven to rescue them and becomes entangled in their problems. And if the situation doesn't turn out well for his associate, the Caretaker feels guilty and responsible, further enmeshing him in drama.

Caretaker Behaviors

Cheerfully ready to tackle any assignment, the Caretaker appears to have an open calendar and limitless energy. In reality, he often misjudges his capabilities and overcommits himself. Also, he struggles to distinguish between empowering leaders and controlling ones, so he'll address all requests equally, without prioritizing. The Caretaker can easily become reactive, responding to the most vocal demand in his constant battle to please others and avoid confrontation. Inevitably, he will miss deadlines and disappoint his teammates. He'll then apologize profusely and redouble his efforts, but will remain stuck on an ever-faster treadmill of unfinished activities.

At Riva, Candace, the Customer Service and Quality Assurance manager, couldn't tell which priorities were most important. She reassigned staff to please Theresa in getting out a product release, frustrating Sam. Then, she traveled to work with a disgruntled client to please Sam, frustrating Foster. At the Highline meeting, she volunteered to take a salary cut, frustrating her team members. For many Caretakers, this "circle of pleasing" eventually leads to frustration on the part of all parties.

Thirsty for any recognition and appreciation, the Caretaker will exhaust himself working long hours in demanding situations. Eager to demonstrate his rock-like invincibility, he will often sacrifice his health or personal relationships rather than become the weak link.

In time, without the mandate from a boss or advisor to recharge his batteries, he will experience some kind of crash, ranging from entitled or pouting behavior to an emotional or physical breakdown.

Drawn to the neediness and suffering of others, the Caretaker feels compelled to take away the pain, rescuing his needy coworkers (Complainers) and calming his agitated ones (Cynics and Controllers). Although this behavior sounds gracious, it actually does more harm than good. Because the Caretaker assumes more than his fair share of responsibility for a problem, he denies others the opportunity to take any credit for it, including their part in its creation and solution. By supposedly helping his teammates, the Caretaker can actually stunt their growth and hurt the organization. Star employees will go elsewhere if they see no possibilities for advancement, causing high turnover—a problem Candace faces in her department.

Striving to be the likeable nice guy, the Caretaker will adopt the image best received by others. He will hesitate to impose consequences for broken agreements and will instead overlook the breach, do the repair work himself, or give the other party "one more chance." By endorsing suboptimal behavior in this way, Caretakers essentially breed lose-lose codependence in the workplace.

Many Caretakers "give themselves away" and hit the wall. When this happens, they often devolve into Complainers, bemoaning how much they care for the organization, how they are unappreciated, and other Complainer-like whining. They become Martyrs, caught in the Caretaker–Complainer loop and bravely "suffering for the cause."

When this burnout happens, cheerful volunteerism is replaced with resignation. Most Complainer-Caretaker Martyrs are torn, wanting to be the good soldier who serves others selflessly, while simultaneously wanting acknowledgment: "[Sigh] It's so hard. No one understands how much I care for this organization or how hard I'm working. But, the work has to be done, and I'm the only one who can do it. I'll just have to persevere and make sure it all works out. [Violins please . . .] You can count on me."

Sometimes the Caretaker and Cynic combine to form the Bitter Soldier, who smothers others with his supposed care for well-being. He steps in to do the actual work, but only after lots of fanfare about his love for the team, while concurrently instilling guilt or implying incompetence in his teammates. This might show up as a variation of "I just want you to be okay. I give all of myself to you [or the team], because you're too vulnerable, weak, and immature to do it on your own. Don't worry, I'll protect you. [But only after telling you how much I'm suffering.]"

This Bitter Soldier variation of the Caretaker frequently demeans coworkers while proclaiming his devotion to the cause ("I have to do it because you're too weak [or too stupid], and I need to protect you . . . and then I'll go back to my lonely silo and suffer.")

Many Caretakers also have a big Controller streak. They might delegate to others, but often with poor or incomplete instructions, setting up either teammates or subordinates for failure so they can proudly enter the scene as the hero and "save the day."

This heroic Caretaker-Controller often comes across as the Benevolent Autocrat: "I have to protect you . . . from yourself. You need my help . . . and you're going to take it!" He likes setting up dependencies in others, establishing himself as the indispensable leader of a group, and blocking any training or empowerment of others.

The Benevolent Autocrat often micromanages his team under the ruse of "I just want you to be successful." Alternatively, he might "sabotage manage," giving subordinates inadequate instructions and setting them up for failure. He can then reenter, like a cartoon superhero, and rescue a floundering subordinate, with the tone of "Yes, I can see this was a tough project for you. Let me handle it for you. [Where would you be without me?]"

COMMON CARETAKER BEHAVIORS

1. Constantly seeking the approval of others
2. Sacrificing personal well-being or happiness for others
3. Avoiding any form of conflict or aggression
4. Struggling with saying "No" to others' requests and taking on too many projects
5. Managing time poorly, overpromising, and then either missing deadlines or underdelivering
6. Assuming more than 100 percent responsibility for problems, enabling continued drama in others
7. Rushing to the aid of others and stunting their emotional and professional growth
8. Setting weak boundaries, or none at all

Managing Caretakers

Caretakers offer substantial gifts to an organization. Genuinely concerned for the well-being of others, they can be cheerful enthusiasts, ever gracious to those around them. As accomplished peacemakers, they know how to bring people together in harmony. Caretakers have great potential for collaboration. When appropriately coached and supported, they can learn to shed their enabling patterns, nurture themselves, and take appropriate responsibility, making their gifts even more substantial.

THE CARETAKER SUBORDINATE OR PEER

Because Caretakers long to feel accepted, validated, and worthy, it is best to create an environment of appreciation and affirmation for them. Praise them often for their efforts and commitment, but watch yourself. If you take too soft an approach, they might easily fall back into their enabling patterns. If you're too hard, they might drift into either Complainer or Cynic behaviors, spinning into helplessness or hopelessness.

Your greatest coaching challenge will probably center on helping Caretakers set and uphold limits. This is perhaps the most difficult growth area for them, given their deep desire to be liked.

When a recovering Caretaker does start drawing boundaries, others will likely either resent or blame him, particularly if he has developed the reputation as the go-to person during crises. Their negative reaction will undoubtedly cause him a great deal of stress at first, but explain to him that by taking on his associates' responsibilities, he is actually endorsing poor behavior and stunting their career growth.

Also, impress upon him that if he doesn't create some kind of balance, he'll burn out and everyone will lose, especially him. So, although you welcome his dedication in taking on new projects and tough challenges, you value and appreciate him even more for completing fewer projects well and on time rather than poorly balancing many. This is particularly important with Complainer-Caretaker Martyrs.

Most Caretakers struggle with managing their time, so work with them to prioritize their action items. Since their to-do list is normally too long and unachievable, you might encourage them to eliminate a bottom percentage (say, one-third). Anticipate defensiveness, fed by their fear of others' anger or rejection if they stop enabling. Inspire and support them to boldly enter this unfamiliar terrain of prioritization.

Caretakers also have difficulty monitoring their own capacity. As you guide them, give them assignments in measureable, bite-size chunks, with regular milestones. Insist that they check in with you before taking on any new projects.

A word of caution: Don't be fooled by the Caretaker's pleasant persona. Bitter Soldiers and Benevolent Autocrats can have colleagues switch between admiring them and resenting them. They might overcommit and deliver subpar work or miss deadlines. They'll then fall into a blend of blaming and apologetics, while committing to redouble their efforts. This is where you must stay clearheaded, empathizing with their situation while imposing clear consequences just as you would with any other subordinate. Model the candid, direct behavior you expect them to adopt.

TIPS FOR COACHING CARETAKER SUBORDINATES OR PEERS

1. Praise them *publicly* for the timely completion of projects.

2. Praise them *privately* for making tough people decisions or drawing hard boundaries.

3. Evaluate late or failed projects. Guide them into seeing how their overcommitment actually hurt the team.

4. Demand intermediate, measureable milestones on projects. Applaud them for proactively approaching you when course corrections are needed.

5. Receive their appreciation of you graciously, whether or not you think you deserve it. Your receipt of this gift helps them feel validated and recognized.

6. Balance corrective statements with sincere positives. Stay upbeat, continually affirming your support for them.

7. Add your ideas during brainstorming sessions, but encourage them to make—and then own—the final decision.

THE CARETAKER BOSS

Caretaker bosses are by nature open and pliable. As such, you can approach them directly, but also in a spirit of kindness and encouragement. Help them delegate and empower others, including you, by offering to take things off their plate. Caretakers are so prone to smother or rescue that you must explicitly ask for additional responsibility. Negotiate clear agreements with intermediate evaluation points. If your supervisor meddles in your projects out of his desire to help, gently tell him you'll happily share your progress at the next review meeting. As you exceed his expectations, he'll give you more autonomy. But watch out: Don't become a Caretaker yourself.

As you do with subordinates, commend Caretaker bosses for setting boundaries and acting decisively, given that they struggle with both. They tend to overanalyze, fearful of making a mistake, and then either look foolish or cause resentment among work associates. You can nudge them into taking small steps toward a tough objective by framing the loss of resources, opportunities, or time that result from inaction. When your Caretaker supervisor does make a decision, underscore in your praise how his choice aligns with his values and the needs of the organization. Trustworthiness and loyalty mean a lot to Caretakers, so they will greatly appreciate your signs of support.

Regarding your career path, you will probably have to be more direct and firm with a Caretaker boss. His desire to please *his* boss could leave you as odd man out and compromise your career plans. Go in with options that are win-win for the company, and then make your case for both career advancement and compensation.

TIPS FOR COACHING CARETAKER BOSSES

1. Show that you appreciate them for setting boundaries and making tough decisions.

2. Offer to take things off their plate—with clear limits.

3. Establish agreements with clear milestones and intermediate metrics. If they meddle, politely say you'll be ready for discussion at the next review cycle, but not now.

4. Show your support, especially during challenging times. Let them know you have their back.

5. Present problems to them along with your recommendations for solving them. Then, offer to take responsibility for implementing the solutions.

6. Take care of yourself. Gently, yet firmly, request what you want in relation to career growth or compensation. Provide a set of options acceptable to you and ask for their commitment to support you.

PART III

Getting Yourself Out of Drama

To manage the four drama types effectively, you must first become drama-free yourself. Only then can you cleanly manage others and guide them toward their own drama-free relationships. Your own grounding in authentic behaviors is the best lead-by-example tool for managing the drama in others.

CHAPTER 7

REVIEW YOUR OWN SCRIPTS

So what do you do when you sense you are falling into drama? The most common reactions are denial ("I'm not angry"), rationalizing ("If you hadn't done _____, I wouldn't be angry"), or blaming ("Of course I'm angry; anybody would be angry after what you did!"). All three are variations of the drama-prone person's classic underlying beliefs: "I'm right" and "It's not my fault." You can choose to be "right," or you can choose to be curious and take responsibility for whatever is happening in your life. Blaming and being right or righteous are familiar and comfortable, but these attitudes are also self-serving and inhibit collaboration. Being curious and taking responsibility, on the other hand, are often unfamiliar and uncomfortable behaviors. They require maturity and vulnerability, and they point the way out of drama to the people around you. Staying entrenched in the need to be right leads to ongoing energy drain, whereas curiosity leads to learning and growth. It's your choice.

When you find yourself slipping into drama or receive feedback that you are slipping into drama, the following four-step process will help you return to a position of openness and curiosity.

Step 1: Take a Time-out: What's *Really* Going On?

When you sense yourself slipping into dramatic behavior, your first action is to stop—literally—even if in mid-sentence. As Einstein said, "You cannot solve a problem from the same consciousness that created it. You must learn to see the world anew." Pause long enough to take a few deep breaths, breaking the rhythm of the moment. Then, check in with your body, a highly accurate barometer of whether you're in drama. Physical sensations such as shallow breathing, stiff neck, sweaty palms, knot in the belly, or tension anywhere in your body are telltale signs that you are falling into drama. At first, you might need to give yourself a few minutes to get centered. As you become more experienced with this technique, however, you will be able to get centered in seconds.

Once you've slowed yourself down, self-reflect and get curious about the triggering dynamic. Become an observer of the situation. Ask yourself, "What's *really* going on here?" Notice the stories you have about another person, group, situation, or yourself: "He's such a jerk," "They don't know what they're doing," "The company's going bankrupt," "I need to save the day." Observe whatever is happening—the undeniable facts, your emotions, and the stories you create—from a place of nonjudgmental curiosity. Shift to a perspective of "Isn't this interesting!"

Many people, especially "fixers," have a hard time taking this observer position. Whenever they sense a problem or disconnection, their first reaction is to jump right in and fix it. They view observing as a form of denial or powerlessness. To guide both yourself and others out of drama, you must resist this urge to fix. Instead, diagnose. Imagine that you are just an advisor, with no vested interest in either the person (in this case, you) or any particular outcome. Explore what spawned this drama in you. What really happened (the facts)? What are you feeling? What opinions are you holding? What story are you concocting? Where do you find yourself wanting to complain, blame, control, or rescue?

As you gain perspective on what's *really* going on, you prepare yourself to get out of drama. If judgments, the need to be right, or the need to fix start to creep back in, repeat this step. Appendix A offers ideas on how to shift out of your initial, emotion-driven responses to the behaviors of dramatic peers.

Step 2: Take Responsibility: What Is Your Part in Creating the Dynamic?

Remember the "hole in the sidewalk" poem? The fastest way to get out of the hole of drama is to acknowledge your own role in it. Say to yourself, "I have a role in creating this drama; it *is* my fault." Accept your own part in creating the troubling situation with all its attendant drama. Explore how you initiated or fueled the situation, and then take healthy responsibility for your part in the dynamic.

This humbling self-examination and acceptance of responsibility is normally very difficult for most of us. Our inner Complainer,

Cynic, and Controller will resist taking any responsibility, preferring to blame others or "the system." On the other hand, our inner Caretaker can take *all* the responsibility for the *entire* dynamic.

Healthy responsibility means owning whatever is upsetting you. No one else is doing it to you. All your internal drama is of your own creation. Ask yourself, "How have I allowed myself to be triggered by others?"

Diligently resist the victim tendency to whine or blame it on others. Nobody can make you feel anything. They simply do what they do, and you feel what you feel. Adopting this mind-set purges any excuses and prepares you for collaborative problem solving with others.

You might feel vulnerable during this step. You'll be tempted to explain why you're right and they're wrong. Your ego might resist strongly, equating responsibility with surrender and being weak. It's easy to get caught in the drama of complaining, self-righteousness, controlling, or rescuing.

But this move into responsibility is a crucial step if you want to exit drama, return to curiosity, and have the potential for collaboration with others. If you start to falter, return to Step 1 or Step 2 and start again.

Step 3: Identify Outcomes:
What Do You Really Want for Yourself?

You've paused to take stock and acknowledge your feelings and judgments. You've taken healthy responsibility for whatever is going on. You have a good grasp of the situation. You're ready to climb out of the hole of drama. Now, *what do you really want for yourself?*

This question has three levels:

1. What do you want?
2. What do you really want?
3. What do you really want for yourself?

The first level of want often focuses on a general situation outside of your control. For example, if you find yourself complaining about unfulfilling work, the answer to the first question might be, "I want the company to give me engaging, important projects." The second level want narrows the scope, but is still outside of your control: "I want my boss to value my efforts and expertise." Both of these wants put responsibility for the solution on someone else.

The healthiest wants are completely within your control, and normally include an element of how you will show up in a specific situation. For example, your answer to the third question might be, "I want to contribute at a level where I feel of value." You have control over the level of your contribution and how you feel. Normally, when all parties (e.g., an executive committee, a partner group, or a project team) get to this third level of want, they find that their desires are compatible. They then have the opportunity to collaborate on solutions in which everyone's core wants are met. But you'll never know until you can surface these core wants. And, as always, it all starts with you.

The table on page 84 provides other examples of these three levels of wants for different situations.

DEEPENING LEVELS OF WANTS			
Situation	What do you want?	What do you really want?	What do you really want for yourself (that you control)?
You feel you're doing all the work.	I want my lazy associates to work harder.	I want teammates who contribute as much as I do.	I want to contribute in a way that I feel provides value and also keeps balance in my life.
A project deadline has been missed.	I don't want the boss to be mad.	I want everyone to pull together so we meet our deadlines.	I want to know that I have given my best to honor the agreements I make.
You've just been passed over for a promotion.	I want to show them why this was a bad decision.	I want a challenging job with commensurate rewards.	I want to grow professionally and be fairly compensated for my contribution.
Drama exists on your team.	I want all the drama to stop.	I want my teammates to collaborate with one another.	I want to model authenticity, work through difficult conversations, and be a catalyst for collaboration.

Step 4: Recommit—Press the Reset Button

Once you are clear on your wants and have taken healthy responsibility for whatever you are experiencing, you can reframe the events of the past as learning experiences, anchor this learning, and then release the past. That was then; this is now. Forgive yourself and those around you; give everyone a fresh start. The longer you wallow in resentment or unforgiveness, the longer you and others will suffer. When you release the past, you reclaim the energy needed to focus clearly on guiding others out of drama and getting what you really want.

Forgiving, however, does not mean forgetting. All life experiences, even detours into drama, are opportunities for learning. While it's still fresh, do an autopsy on your negative patterns—for example, your tendencies to complain, criticize, dominate, or enable. Recall the "hole in the sidewalk" poem. Examine the hole *you* fell into. Where could you have caught this sooner and walked around the hole? Where were your boundaries too weak or too strong? What is the lesson learned?

As you begin to plot your next course of action, shift into curiosity about what *you* can do. Explore how you can shift the situation into something positive. Intentionally choose a new plan and commit to it fully. Affirm yourself for choosing curiosity over drama. Recommit to the authentic behaviors of healthy responsibility, candor, empowerment, and caring.

Learning to correct your own dramatic behavior may be more difficult for you than managing the dramatic behavior in others. Fortunately, in addition to the tools mentioned in this chapter, there are a number of self-discovery tools designed to help you when you find yourself slipping into dramatic behavior. One such analytic tool is presented in Appendix B, and others can be found on our website, **www.DramaFreeOffice.com**. These tools will guide you on your journey of self-discovery and help you detour around the drama holes in your personal sidewalk.

CHAPTER 8

SHIFTING OUT OF YOUR DRAMA

The last chapter presented a self-reflection process for shifting out of your own drama. This chapter shows the application of the process in an all-too-common work example and describes how Laura chose to use the process on herself as she prepared to lead the SWAT team at Riva. But first, let's take a look at a case study from our own experience.

Drama Case Study

Several years ago when I (Jim) was running a technology company, we would hold quarterly brainstorming sessions to reevaluate our strategic marketing. At one of these sessions, I was about twenty minutes into outlining a new program idea when I noticed a more junior product manager rolling his eyes, shaking his head, and regularly looking out the window.

All the drama characters in me started to voice their opinions. My inner Complainer went into a cycle of self-pity. Once again, it was clear that nobody in the organization cared about my ideas. Even though I'm the final decision maker and they might go along with what I want, they don't really believe in me. Why did I even bother to contribute? I bet they all feel like this guy does.

My inner Cynic had a completely different view: My concept is so beyond this bozo it's no wonder he can't understand it. I'm giving him the most innovative idea of the entire session and he's missing it. Since he's obviously not paying attention, I'm going to grill him on the finer points of the concept and make him look like an idiot in front of his peers. Better yet, I'll wait until he presents his thoughts and then shoot holes in his logic.

My Controller was girded for battle. Doesn't this guy know I could fire him in a heartbeat? I'm the boss here! Besides, since I've got the most experience in the room, and it's my company, we don't need to be brainstorming anyway. I know what I want; I know what's best. I'm taking charge here.

And then the inner Caretaker quietly worked over my conscience. If one of our more creative associates has lost interest, I must have really screwed up. This is the brain trust of the company. I'd better rethink my entire idea so they'll like it. I have to get consensus on this, and I'm clearly losing them now. I'll adjourn the meeting and totally rework the presentation.

Meanwhile, all I knew for certain was that the associate was rolling his eyes, looking down, shaking his head, and looking out the window.

The first step was to pause, take a couple breaths, and observe what was going on. Yes, the associate appeared to be bored or disinterested. That was my judgment. I was experiencing a spectrum of emotions, including anger at his behavior and embarrassment that I wasn't getting my point across better. When I was able to navigate the anger and embarrassment and detach from my judgments, I could begin to explore my part in this drama.

I'd been speaking for over twenty minutes. We'd established a guideline at the beginning of the session that all presentations would be ten minutes or less, after which we'd brainstorm as a group. I'd also blitzed them with sixty PowerPoint slides, packed with lots of text. Lots of data, but not very inspirational. As I put myself in their shoes, I could see how they might be both frustrated with me for hijacking the time and overwhelmed with a fire hose of information. I would be!

In addition, I didn't know much about this associate. He might be facing some other personal issue that was distracting him from being fully present at the session.

So what did I want? I wanted this person to wake up and pay attention, and as the boss, I could demand that he do it. He might shift his outward behavior, but I had no direct control over his attention span. Next, I wanted the group to embrace my ideas. Again, while I could shift my presentation style to be more entertaining, I couldn't mandate this. What I really wanted was to model curious, open behavior and make my presentations crisp, accurate, and lighthearted. I could control how I showed up and my attitude and excitement for the process. I could also initiate a conversation with the young associate, asking his counsel on how I might make the presentation of the idea more engaging. I could also review and refine our brainstorming guidelines with the group, getting agreement on the go-forward protocol for our sessions.

Pressing the reset button meant releasing all the judgments conjured up by my inner Complainer, Cynic, Controller, and Caretaker and committing to being an engaged participant in the brainstorming process.

At the actual meeting, I suggested a short break. When everyone returned, I made a joke about "death by PowerPoint" and suggested we move right into brainstorming. The participants were tentative at first, since they knew I hadn't finished the presentation, but gradually they began to feel safer and started making comments. I intentionally expressed appreciation for every idea, even the ones I judged ridiculous, capturing them all on a whiteboard. The seemingly disinterested associate came alive and volunteered an insight that eventually saved us two months' development effort on the project.

How Laura Dealt with Her Own Drama

In the first SWAT team meeting, Laura might have come across as the mature mediator, trying to manage the varied personalities while breeding the collaboration needed to solve a tough business problem. Outwardly, yes. But let's look at what is going on behind the scenes.

The opening chapter described Laura's rise from technician, to department manager, to director of Operations in only three years. Laura worked long hours to get the job done and displayed great loyalty, which served her well as she rose quickly through the ranks. She also has a Caretaker streak, wanting everyone to get along, even if it means she ends up doing most of the work. Her inner Caretaker wants Cliff's approval and is tempted to overpromise on what the team can deliver.

Laura has always been drawn to management and has actively sought leadership roles. While she normally comes across as inspirational and empowering, she also has a Controller part that likes both the recognition that comes from the tough projects and the power to do it any way she wants. By sitting in the driver's seat, she can control the problems, the people responsible, and the solutions. In taking on the Riva project, her inner Controller wants to set very high expectations and oversee every decision.

These Controller-Caretaker tendencies tempt her to micromanage the Riva team and be the heroine in the company. Earlier in her career, it had been hard for her to set clear agreements and delegate. She'd lose patience with—and then do the work for—Complainers and Caretakers, and quickly become resentful or angry around Cynics and Controllers.

But Laura was ahead of the game. During the course of her career, she received coaching and learned how to acknowledge and shift these parts of her that were prone to fall into drama. Now, when situations or individuals "push her buttons" and tempt her to fall into drama, she catches herself and "walks around the hole." The Highline situation tempted her to caretake or control. Let's see how she stayed authentic.

During all the theatrics of the initial team meeting, Laura consciously maintained regular, deep breathing and an unattached position. Unbeknownst to the other team members caught in drama, she kept saying to herself, "Isn't this interesting. I wonder what's really going on here?" After a few stabs at restoring rationality to the meeting, she faced a choice: (1) assume an authoritarian position, cut off venting and blaming, and force discussion on the project or (2) use this first session with the team for data-gathering, knowing that it would delay any work on the project for a precious day. She chose the latter, knowing that she'd have to understand each person's tendencies toward drama to guide them toward authentic interactions if the project were to have any chance of success.

Outwardly calm during the meeting, she was monitoring her

internal feelings and judgments. Her Controller part wanted to reprimand Sam for being such a crybaby and only caring about himself. "Just suck it up and make your numbers," she wanted to say. Theresa's sarcasm made Laura angry, especially when Theresa would hide behind high-tech excuses rather than own up to missed deadlines and cost overruns—at least that was the story floating through Laura's head.

Her Cynic pictured Foster as a windbag bean counter, who talked a good game but was clueless on Riva's operations. She wondered if he had ever really run anything! And Candace's naiveté on management was both ironic and sad. How did she ever get promoted into a management position?

Laura's Caretaker was also quick to jump in. Clearly the team was struggling. They all needed her help. Cliff had trusted her to lead the team and solve the problem, and she'd do whatever it took to gain his approval. Her first job was to mediate all their differences and restore harmony to the team. That would be the heroic thing to do.

As you read this, you might be thinking, "C'mon, she didn't really have those thoughts. Nobody really thinks like that. How could she even function in the meeting?" If you have doubts, check in with yourself during emotional exchanges or intense meetings. Keep a log of both your feelings (resentment, anxiety, anger, worry, guilt, sadness, etc.) and judgments (incompetence, arrogance, bullying, pity, etc.) about others. Our experience is that almost everyone has a continuous stream of feelings and judgments that, if unchecked, will take over your thinking, corrupt any chance of collaboration, and cast you into drama.

Back to Laura. How did she use the four-step process to stay authentic with the Riva team during the initial meeting?

Her first step was to mentally detach herself from the drama dynamics of the individuals. She took a few deep breaths. She noticed her rising anger and frustration and the stories she had created about her associates: Sam being a crybaby, Theresa hiding behind technology, Foster as a windbag, and Candace's naiveté. She also noticed her own inclination to disband the team and do everything herself.

From this unattached perspective, she could notice these feelings and judgments without acting on them. From this observer position, she could ask herself the tough question, "What responsibility do I have in creating this fiasco of a meeting?" Her first answer was, "I'm not responsible. They're the ones acting like spoiled children." This reaction is common because it's so easy to place blame on others and absolve ourselves of any culpability. But as she continued to reflect, she began to acknowledge that she had done little homework on the behavioral patterns of the four team members. Nor had she met with them individually before this launch meeting to set both her expectations for the group and her expectations for each individual.

In her mind, again hidden from the theatrics of the Riva team, Laura took ownership of both her judgments of the individuals and her part in creating the dysfunctional meeting. She shed her rationalizations and simply acknowledged to herself, "Okay, I did a poor job of setting expectations. And I could have asked sharper questions to run it better in the moment." From this place of detachment and ownership, she could get a clear picture of what she wanted.

Moving to the third step—identifying what she really wanted— she realized that her knee-jerk desire was for her four associates to grow up and act like mature managers. This was clearly outside of her control. She then pondered what she really wanted: a collaborating team focused on solving the Highline situation. While more positive in tone and within her sphere of influence, this was still outside of her control. She then thought about what she really wanted for herself. Having released the judgments and emotions around the meeting drama, the answer became clear: She wanted to focus her energies on optimizing the potential for team interaction. She wanted to set aside her own biases for controlling and rescuing, and learn about the nuances of the individuals and the team. Then, she could guide them individually, mediate discussions in the group, and give them the best possible chance of solving the Highline customer service problem.

In a nutshell, she wanted to show up authentically, have unambiguous agreements with each of the team members, and lead clearly. All were fully under her control and exactly what the team needed.

Laura smiled internally as she noticed how she'd allowed herself, at least for a moment, to get sucked into the team's collective drama.

And she let it all go.

She could now focus completely on realizing her big want: show up authentically, get clear agreements with each of the team members about her expectations, and then lead the project.

We've taken a few pages to describe how Laura navigated her own drama. The entire process played out in Laura's head in less than a minute, hidden from the other SWAT team members. You might be thinking, "How did she do it?" or more important, "How can I do this?"

Commit to Authenticity and Self-Awareness

Earlier in Laura's career when she was burning herself out in her job and alienating others with her need to control, a wise business associate took her aside and asked if she was open to some candid observations. He pointed out how, in his judgment, her behaviors would eventually limit her career growth, and that she was headed toward burnout. He encouraged her to take stock of her life and get clear on what she really wanted—for herself. He then expressed his belief in her as a person and leader.

At first, she was defensive, full of rationalizations, and even a little angry. But she recognized an intrinsic authenticity in this respected person and she reflected on his suggestions. After a few tries, she settled on her core want: to be an authentic leader with a life outside of the office. This really resonated with her—she just had no idea how to make it happen. Feeling a little scared and vulnerable, she approached the wise associate, told him her core want, and asked if he would be willing to mentor her in the process. He smiled and agreed, and he began to advise her in both authentic leadership and authentic living. She learned the attributes of authenticity: take healthy responsibility for her life, be creative and collaborative in her interactions, empower her subordinates, care for others without rescuing them, and approach all of her life with both curiosity and openness.

Of course, she occasionally drifted into drama, but as shown in the Highline meeting, she acknowledged and took responsibility for the drifts, forgave herself, and reaffirmed her commitment to authentic leadership.

If you are interested in finding a mentor, consider the following list of attributes as a guide.

WHAT TO LOOK FOR IN MENTORS

- They have a way of being that you admire. They walk their talk.
- Their lives are grounded in honesty, compassion, patience, and discipline.
- They are neither intimidated nor intimidating.
- They have the wisdom to know when to stay in the background and let things unfold, and when to be decisive in the moment.
- They have a highly developed intuition. They can conceive new approaches to fit an emerging situation.
- They can quickly get to the heart of problems and speak the hard truths.
- They can "hold the space" for you to express your thoughts and emotions safely.
- They treat confidentiality as sacred.
- They are committed to their own ongoing personal growth and holistic health.
- They have their own "personal advisory board" for guidance and accountability.
- When they drift into unproductive behaviors, they shift back quickly with integrity.
- They take themselves lightly; they can laugh at themselves.

If you wish to anchor authenticity as a way of life, you must also commit to learning as much as you can about yourself. This includes your intrinsic personality type, your inventory of core values, your signature strengths, your preferred style of leadership, and, of course, your most common ways of falling into drama. Most of these self-exploration areas are beyond the scope of this book. Our website, **www.DramaFreeOffice.com**, references the best authors and online assessments for these self-exploration categories. We've used both the approaches of these authors and the online assessments with hundreds of coaching clients who seek both greater self-awareness and a deeper engagement with life. They work.

PART IV

Guiding Others Out of Drama

Perhaps you need to solve a problem, like the Highline crisis, that requires crisp teamwork. Or maybe your subordinates are entrenched in dramatic behavior and are resisting your coaching. Maybe your boss is stuck in his own "hole in the sidewalk" that limits your productivity and demoralizes your team. In these drama-laden situations, you need to address your associates one-on-one with the goal of developing a personal rapport and obtaining a commitment to replace their dramatic behaviors with open, curious ones. The following chapters outline the tools for addressing these energy-draining situations.

CHAPTER 9

THE TOOLS FOR DEFUSING DRAMA

As a manager, you must clearly state the behavior you expect and the results you seek. As presented in part III, an authentic, drama-free frame of mind will give you the best chance of doing this with calmness and candor. When you confront your associates, remember that it's not your job to fix anyone. And while it might be nice, it's irrelevant whether the drama king or queen likes you. This chapter presents five proven tools for gaining another person's commitment to collaborative, drama-free behavior: having the direct conversation, delivering ultimatums, handling emotion, making clear agreements, and offering appreciation.

Your tool selection and approach to dealing with different people will vary depending on the manifestation of their drama. The following table contrasts healthy and unhealthy ways to deal with drama in your associates.

APPROACHING DIFFERENT DRAMA TYPES		
PHYSICAL HEALTH ISSUE	**UNHEALTHY APPROACH**	**HEALTHY APPROACH**
Hangnail	Hand amputation	Clippers and file
Pneumonia	Aspirin	Penicillin
FORM OF DRAMA	**UNHEALTHY APPROACH**	**HEALTHY APPROACH**
Complainer	Ultimatums	Guiding them to be more decisive
Cynic	Browbeating	Focusing on possibilities
Controller	Cowering	Holding boundaries and teaching them to delegate
Caretaker	Piling on work	Helping them develop boundaries
All forms of drama	Ignoring	Having the direct conversation

Having the Direct Conversation

Let's assume that you (like Laura) have prepared for an encounter with a drama-prone associate. Grounded in your own maturity and clarity, you can initiate a conversation around the person's behavior. The format for the conversation with someone you believe can change their behavior is outlined in The Direct-Conversation

Model on page 104. In a succinct manner, lay out the five elements that are key to any direct exchange:

1. Observable facts around the energy-draining behavior
2. Judgments, evaluations, or stories you make up about the individual and the situation
3. Your emotions regarding the dynamic
4. Your part in creating the dynamic
5. What you want—both from the other individual and for yourself

Once you present the situation, you can't predict how others will respond. Ideally, they will listen with curiosity, mirror back what they heard, honor your emotions, and keep their own perspective in check. You can then proceed to brainstorm creative solutions to the issues. But don't count on it. Usually, drama-prone people will compose their defenses as you speak, be incapable of reflecting back your position, and either launch immediately into a counterattack or retreat into silence.

During this whole process, regardless of the other person's response, your vital role as manager is to listen and reflect back with the goal of truly understanding his views. You don't have to agree; just understand. As you peel the onion of his suppressed judgments and feelings—in a caring fashion—he might begin to relax his position and open the door for collaborative discourse. As you model curiosity and vulnerability, you give him the opportunity to do the same. When you refuse to engage in a battle of words, you invite him to set aside his need to be right, making it possible to engage in a respectful way.

THE DIRECT-CONVERSATION MODEL

HOW TO PRESENT THE SITUATION

- **Define the positive intention of the interaction.**
  (For example, "I want to work more effectively with you.")

- **"I have a situation I'd like to discuss with you. Is now a good time?"** *(If not, agree on a time.)*

- **"The specific facts are . . ."** *(Recordable facts, not judgments)*

- **"I believe that . . ."** *(I think . . . ; In my opinion . . . ; My judgment is . . . ; I can imagine that . . . ; I make up a story that . . .)*

- **"I feel . . ."** *(An emotion: sad, angry, scared, ashamed, guilty, excited, numb, happy)*

- **"My part in this is . . ."** *(Share your role in creating or sustaining the situation. Healthy responsibility demands that each person take 100 percent responsibility for the situation.)*

- **"And I specifically want . . ."** *(It's important to be precise. What do you want for yourself, for the organization, and from the other person?)*

HOW TO REFLECT BACK

- **"Let me see if I understand you . . ."** *(Reflect or paraphrase without interpretation; seek to truly understand without rebuttal.)*

- **"Is that accurate?"** *(If not, reflect again.)*

- **"Is there more?"** *(This is a crucial question. Ask in a kind, genuine, and curious voice. If there is more, repeat the process until the presenter is satisfied and the emotions are dissipated.)*

- **"What do you really want?"** *(Ask in a kind, genuine, and curious voice. Align the person's desire with a larger goal to lay the groundwork for true collaboration.)*

- **Appreciate the person.** *(Tell him you value his willingness to engage in discussion and seek an authentic relationship with you and the group. Commit to working with him to sustain the progress made in this session.)*

At some point in the conversation, you'll probably discover that both of you want some version of the same thing, perhaps (1) to feel valued in the organization, in work teams, and in one-on-one interactions, or (2) to be productive and efficient. Most people would also like to have some fun at work! When you agree on these core wants, and perhaps others more specific to your situation, you can begin developing a positive go-forward relationship.

AN EXAMPLE OF A DIRECT CONVERSATION

We facilitate direct conversations with almost every team with which we work. You have likely been thinking of your own uses for the tool—with a single employee or with a team.

Some instances of direct conversation seem simple on the surface, but their implications can be huge.

There was a woman whom we'll call Sue working for an IT director whom we'll name Jerry. While initially withdrawn and displaying many cynical behaviors, after her direct conversation, she was engaged, committed, and creative. It might surprise you that it was Sue who initiated the conversation with her superior.

While the conversation flowed more smoothly in real life, the steps of the direct conversation were as follows:

Sue's affirmation to Jerry: "Jerry, I want to have this conversation with you because this company means a lot to me. I've invested many years of my career in the success of the company, and there's an issue hindering my engagement that I want to clear up. Is now a good time?"

Jerry was concerned about the situation. Even more important, he cared about Sue. He had noticed her slumped posture and withdrawn nature over the prior week and was grateful for her effort to initiate conversation.

"Yes," he replied.

Facts: "My laptop broke two weeks ago, and it hasn't been fixed or replaced. IT provided me with a loaner laptop that was very slow and had only rudimentary software."

Judgment: "I think the IT process is slow, and I think it impedes our work."

Emotion: "I feel frustrated, and a little angry that it's been two weeks."

My part: "I chose not to confront IT about both the inadequate loaner and the status of my own computer's repair. I just waited, hoping you'd eventually contact me."

Specific request: "I want my computer situation handled. More broadly, I want broken computers to be repaired or replaced within forty-eight hours."

As Sue spoke Jerry leaned forward in his chair. He truly wanted to understand and address Sue's issue. He noticed when his own defensiveness started to arise and took a deep breath instead of making excuses. Knowing that jumping to conclusions was ineffective, he responded, making sure to reflect back Sue's statements: "Sue, let me see if I understand. You turned in your laptop a couple of weeks ago and still haven't gotten it fixed or replaced. Sounds like you haven't gotten any information about it. You were given a loaner laptop that is quite slow and has only basic software. Being without a high-speed, fully-loaded computer is impeding your work, and the longer it takes, the more frustrated you get. You acknowledge that you could have been more proactive—checking on the situation rather than waiting. And what you really want is for the computer to be fixed."

Before anything else, Jerry checked himself. He knew that he was sensitive about IT—it was his baby—and that he sometimes heard criticism that wasn't actually there. He checked his Complainer tendencies and committed to stay mature. He thought he'd done a good job, but something didn't seem quite right. "Is that accurate?" he asked.

Sue maintained eye contact. "It is accurate," she answered.

Jerry looked at Sue earnestly. He was thankful for her insight into his department and team. Still, he couldn't shake the intuition that this wasn't the real issue. "Is there more? I mean, is there something additional or deeper that's bothering you?" Jerry asked.

Sue was impressed with Jerry's listening abilities. Through his posture, the accuracy of his reflection, and his intonation, she knew that he was engaged. Because she felt more confident with him, she decided to address the real issue. The computer *was* important. And her description of the situation *was* accurate. But these were the outward symptoms—the rational pieces she could identify. She decided to take a risk and share another layer of the story.

"There is more," she confessed. "As you know, I work from home part-time and I travel frequently. Many people in our company do. My laptop is the only way I can do that work. I've been interpreting the delay in getting mine fixed as a message, essentially telling me that I'm not needed or valued. I've made myself very scared over this, and have even begun thinking I need to start looking for a new job."

She took a deep breath. "Saying this out loud, I feel vulnerable and exposed. I'm worried you'll confirm that I'm not needed, or that I'll sound paranoid for having the thought. But I decided this was worth it. Living in the uncertainty was worse!

"Practically, I could have been more creative in my working

arrangements," Sue continued. "Emotionally, I see that I withdrew when I started to think that. A cynical part of me started to show up more—which makes me a much less desirable team member. There were many times when I could have shifted to more productive behaviors and didn't. So I definitely contributed in making this worse.

"I guess what I really want is your vote of confidence in my work. I need more affirmation that my contribution matters. I'm open to constructive criticism, too. Your feedback on my performance would make a big difference. And a fully-functioning computer to make that contribution is really just the mechanism for my underlying need to feel valued for my work—which I guess is my deeper want."

Jerry took a deep breath. This made sense to him. All the behaviors he'd seen from Sue stemmed from her fear. His concern that the computer wasn't the real issue was validated. He replied, "Sue, I'm impressed with you bringing this to my attention. I also appreciate your courage in speaking about the real issue, beyond the computer repair. Let me make sure I've fully grasped your experience." He reflected her underlying issue back to her.

"Because you do work remotely, you interpreted the delay in getting your laptop back as an unspoken message that you were not valuable to the organization—so much so that you considered looking for work elsewhere. You felt scared. And in sharing this with me, you feel vulnerable and exposed. In retrospect, you believe more creative working arrangements, more proactive ways to change the situation, and an attitude adjustment—from cynicism and withdrawal to candid collaboration—would have helped. And now you want me to be more vocal about your performance so you know where you stand. And, assuming you are still wanted, you'd like to get your computer back so you can continue your outstanding performance."

They both smiled. Sue preempted his question. "That's exactly right. I feel so much better. I appreciate you taking the time to really understand my position—even if I might have appeared overly concerned. I know that if we were able to get through this conversation, we can work out something as relatively simple as a computer!"

They then began to brainstorm IT fixes, communication strategies, remote working arrangements, and performance feedback systems.

Delivering Ultimatums

Often, high-drama people are simply incapable of engaging in a respectful dialogue. They've developed such strong listening filters that they can't hear what you're saying and remain caught in their emotions and their need to be right. They might entrench themselves even further in defensive postures, become passive-aggressive, or, in extreme cases, even become volatile. Collaboration or negotiation with these behaviors is a waste of time. If the person is a subordinate, you might need to place her on probationary status with an explicit performance plan or contract for her to retain her position.

Tailor your presentation of an ultimatum to make sure the person fully understands it, and stay crystal clear about your expectations going forward. Commit to staying unattached, firm, and matter-of-fact in your delivery. If you are at all concerned about your physical or emotional safety, insist that another person be present. Capture all discussed areas in a written summary.

If an ultimatum is necessary, be cordial in your interactions, but detach from the relationship emotionally, particularly if the other person's drama tends to trigger your own. Isolate him as much as possible from other associates and act swiftly on breaches of his agreements.

Even though relationship authenticity seems unlikely once you've gotten to the point of having to issue an ultimatum, remain open to a turnaround in your associate's behavior. Some immature, drama-prone personalities have never had any boundaries imposed on them. This is actually common among bright high-achievers who are used to acting autonomously. Your clear, enforced boundaries might be just the catalyst such individuals need to grow up. Stay open-minded and supportive, yet firm, and be quick to show appreciation for positive movement. Your authenticity might inspire the person into becoming a valuable part of your team.

AN EXAMPLE OF AN ULTIMATUM

Alan started out as a great employee. He progressed quickly—maybe too quickly for his skill set—through the ranks at the advertising firm where he led client relations. Tom, his manager, had become frustrated with the number of mistakes Alan had been making. He would send client materials to the wrong address, misspell customer names, or confuse the media outlet they were using. Tom used the appropriate HR channels to track the mistakes.

Even more concerning to Tom, Alan had begun to display many Complainer behaviors. Nothing was his fault—his computer system had messed up or the operations group fed him faulty information. He dodged accountability or blamed others for his mistakes. Initially, Tom's Caretaker part was triggered. He went overboard on his coaching and even double-checked routine work. When he realized that he was doing the accuracy-checking work *for* Alan, he became angry and noticed his Controller part wanting to chastise Alan. "*How can he be so lazy and stupid?*" he raged in his thoughts.

Alan repeatedly broke his agreements, and he wasn't responding to coaching. Tom realized he had to take more drastic action. He also was aware of his tendencies to both rescue and micromanage. He knew that he couldn't wait any longer for things to change.

Instead, he committed to authenticity. Rather than resenting Alan, he chose to clearly express his expectations. He sat down to write the ultimatum. After several drafts, he was ready. He scheduled a time and invited Alan into his office.

Tom remembered to breathe as he spoke. "Alan, I have a serious topic I want to cover with you. I want you to listen all the way through before you respond. As you listen, I want you to consider whether you can do this or not. This is a yes/no decision. There is no room for negotiation here."

Alan started to retort. "This isn't fair! Have you been talking with Operations?"

Tom interrupted, "Alan, this is exactly the kind of behavior I am talking about. I want you to listen all the way through before you respond. And then, I want you to think carefully before you respond."

Alan nodded.

"We've documented the mistakes with your client work at a rate of about one per week. More distressing to me is your attitude. Whenever one of these errors arises, you are quick to tell me who, besides you, is to blame for this. From today forward, the rate of mistakes must drop to no more than one per quarter. Equally important, when something happens—mistakes, miscommunications, or anything outside the realm of routine interactions—I want you to start the conversation with, 'This is my responsibility because . . .' And I want you to identify what you will do to solve it.

"Specifically, if you fail to let me know about a mistake or missed deadline, if I hear you say, 'There's nothing I can do,' or if I find the same mistake in your work twice, we will end the three-month probationary period I'm putting you on, and you will need to find a new place to work.

"Do you understand?"

Alan flushed red. He looked like he was hunched in his chair in silent protest.

Tom repeated, "Alan, do you understand?"

"Yeah, I get it," Alan responded.

"Good," Tom said. "I'll prepare a written summary of this conversation for you to review and sign within twenty-four hours."

Handling Emotion

On occasion, either during a direct conversation or when you're delivering an ultimatum, your associates might become even more defensive and rooted in their positions of victimhood, cynicism, control, or rescuing. They might also fall into visible emotion: tears, blushing, frustration, or anger. Your first reaction might be to fix ("It's all going to be okay"), deny ("This is really nothing to be upset about"), backpedal ("Gee, I'm sorry you're taking it that way"), or retaliate ("Oh yeah, well I'm pretty mad about this, too!"). However, rather than easing the emotion, these responses will probably escalate it.

Whatever else you do, acknowledge and honor what you see in the other person: "I notice some tears [or you've gone silent] [or you're looking out the window]. How are you feeling now?" or "What's going on for you right now?" Then, listen and reflect using the tools listed on page 115.

When people become emotional, most questions will take them out of their feelings and into their head. Since you're seeking dialogue and collaboration, this might seem desirable, but it will actually push the unexpressed emotions back inside, where they inhibit or sabotage collaboration. So, when emotion is present, avoid asking any questions other than "What's going on for you right now?"

Reflecting can take several forms. The simplest and often safest approach is to mirror back exactly what emotional people say. For example, if they say, "I feel I have no value anymore in the organization," you might reflect back, "I understand that you feel you have no value anymore in the organization." To a dispassionate observer, this parroting may seem demeaning, but the person experiencing the emotion will actually appreciate that you fully understood their experience. If you feel confident in your understanding, you may paraphrase their expression. For example, in the situation above, you might say, "You don't feel important in your current role within the company."

It also helps to acknowledge their perspective by saying something like, "As I put myself in your position, I can see how you might feel that you have no value in the organization." This does not mean you *agree* with their position, but rather that you understand how they feel. This validation breeds safety and effectively defuses emotion.

As the emotion starts to pass, gently ask, "Is there more?" and continue reflecting until the person feels completely heard. Then, look for an opportunity to collaborate by asking, "What would you like to have happen now?" His answer will determine whether you start exploring options right away or defer to a later date. Be ready to set aside your agenda if your colleague isn't ready. You might compare calendars and agree on another time to have a collaborative discussion. This honors his in-the-moment fragility, while still signaling that the issue is important to you and that you're committed to getting resolution.

If you do proceed with the conversation, reestablish a connection with him by asking, "What would support for you look like?" Know your boundaries when you do this, especially if your Caretaker tendencies are triggered. You don't have to agree to deliver on his request. If you can't comply, reflect back the request, explain that it's not possible, and open the door for alternatives: For example, "I hear you'd like another three weeks on the project. Although that's not an option, I'm willing to brainstorm other forms of support."

On rare occasions, the other person might become overly agitated or even unstable. If you anticipate this as even a remote possibility, invite a third party to join you for the conversation and be prepared to stop at the first signs of volatility. If you're alone and emotions escalate, end the discussion as calmly as possible and go to a safe place. You can then evaluate your options with a Human Resources professional.

HOW TO ADDRESS VISIBLE EMOTION

- Show that you're picking up on the person's behaviors that often signal unexpressed emotions: "I notice _____ [an observable behavior]."

- Give the person an opening to express his feelings: "What's coming up for you?"

- In general, avoid asking data-gathering questions. Especially avoid asking "why" questions. They drive people back into their heads, short-circuit the emotional expression, and delay any collaboration.

- Reflect or reframe: "Let me see if I understand you: _____" or "It sounds to me like _____."

- Honor their perspective: "When I put myself in your position, I can understand why you feel _____."

- Continue to ask "Is there more?" until the person feels heard.

- Seek to reestablish a connection: "What would support for you look like?"

- Look for an opening to collaborate: "What would you like to have happen now?"

- If you feel threatened, immediately end the conversation and go to a safe place. Your physical and emotional safety is top priority.

Making Clear Agreements

Whether you are managing collaborative associates or drama-prone ones, you must define what will be done, who will do it, and when it must be completed. Precise, measureable agreements are the most important tool for efficient, productive interactions. Even mature colleagues sometimes miss opportunities to make clear agreements and fall into drama due to misunderstandings or misperceptions. All the drama characters—Complainer, Cynic, Controller, and Caretaker—will resist such agreements because they remove ambiguity, and saboteurs don't like to be boxed in.

The level of collaboration and flexibility in agreements depends on the maturity of the other parties. As a general rule, higher-drama people—the ones who will resist the most—require more explicit agreements. When in doubt, err on the side of being overly specific. The table on the next page outlines the general approach for making clear agreements.

If the direct conversation goes well and you establish a go-forward agreement, immediately affirm the positive movement. The best way to anchor the progress with *any* drama type is through specific recognition and appreciation. As your colleagues sustain mature, curious behaviors, enlist their active involvement in crafting solutions to issues. One of the greatest satisfactions in management is coaching drama-prone individuals to become open-minded team players.

In chapter 11 we'll see how Laura establishes clear agreements with each of the Highline team members on how they will commit to interact within the project team.

MAKING CLEAR AGREEMENTS

- State specifically what you want the person to do—*not* what you don't want: "I want your two departments to engage in brainstorming sessions that yield at least three creative new options" versus "I don't want to see your departments fighting with each other."

- Define how you will measure success, and use a numeric parameter (e.g., new options offered, financial metrics, sales achieved, bugs fixed, calls answered).

- Provide a precise deadline for completion (e.g., work must be done by Monday morning).

- Establish intermediate, measureable milestones to track progress and to allow for course corrections if you sense agreements are being broken.

- Keep working until the other party signals agreement. Listen for a clear response from one of three alternatives:
  - The person accepts: "I agree. I'll be glad to do it for you."
  - He declines respectfully: "I have reflected on your request, and *I choose* not to do it for you." With mature associates, you can brainstorm other options, but with less mature associates, you'll likely have to issue an ultimatum.
  - He declines and presents a counteroffer: "I can make the new agreement, but only if I'm able to renegotiate a prior one." Then, you can collaborate and negotiate.

Appreciation

A core human need is to feel recognized and valued. Even the most jaded cynic has a part of him that longs to be appreciated. When we feel valued by others, we're more inclined to want to earn and retain their approval and respect.

The act of appreciation is simply telling others what we like about them or their behaviors—catching them doing something good. The most effective appreciation is specific, timely, and sincere.

Appreciation can be offered in several forms. Perhaps the most effective is the face-to-face expression of gratitude. The further you have to travel, the more effective and lasting the appreciation. One time I (Jim) flew across the country for a thirty-minute meeting with an old friend and mentor. He's an internationally recognized guide to thousands of people. At the end of our time together, he remarked that in the past fifteen years, only two other people had visited him simply to express their appreciation. Our relationship skyrocketed to a new level. Whether you're flying cross-country or walking to an adjacent office space, the face-to-face recognition of another person will often make his day and strengthen your relationship with him.

The next most effective appreciation is the hand-addressed, handwritten note. Notice the difference in how you feel when opening a personalized, handwritten holiday card compared with a mass-mailed, embossed-signature holiday card. One of the most sought-after speakers and leadership coaches in America sends out ten to twenty personalized cards to friends, associates, clients, and colleagues each week.

In the workplace, the note can be as simple as a sticky note placed on the person's desk or computer monitor. You don't have to write a sonnet. The message can be as simple as "John, your sense of humor and insights on [something specific] led to real breakthroughs at the meeting today. Way to go!"

A spontaneous appreciation phone call will often make another person's day. It doesn't have to be long: "Hi, Ian. Just wanted to thank you for your patience today at the meeting as we slogged through the financials. I know this isn't your favorite way to spend time, but I noticed how you stayed attentive and asked some really good questions about [something specific]. This really meant a lot to me. Thanks."

E-mailed appreciation is also effective if highly personalized and short. Consider that the recipient might be getting hundreds of e-mails a day. To get his attention, the subject line has to carry the heart of your appreciation—perhaps something like "Thanks for your candor at today's meeting" or "Your insights on [something specific] were outstanding." No matter how effusive you choose to be in the body of the e-mail, plan on the recipient only reading the subject line.

It sounds easy. Catch people doing something good. Find something you like about another person and tell him. But if appreciation is so easy and effective, what prevents us from lavishing it on others?

A common resistance to offering appreciation is the myth that you'll look fake or insincere. This is a possibility if the appreciative comment is generic—for example, "You're a great guy" or "Good meeting today." You might also be perceived as insincere if you have not been prone to offer appreciations in the past. If your personality is more reserved, others might think, "Whoa, what happened to Chris? He must have taken a happy pill this morning." You might be teased or even diminished.

Another block to giving appreciation is that many people have a hard time receiving it. They'll discount or reject your comments, or they'll become self-deprecating. You might wonder why you should bother if they're not going to openly receive your appreciation anyway. But keep appreciating in spite of your hesitation. Even if others seem to discount you or reject the appreciation, something positive is likely getting through to them. If you commit to being consistently sincere and specific in your appreciation, their old views of you will gradually begin to shift.

Other common reasons for not offering appreciation include: they'll become arrogant; they'll come to expect it; or they'll feel I'm becoming weak or too touchy-feely. But in most workplace environments, these are lame excuses for not taking the risk to acknowledge the positive behaviors of others.

One of the best reasons for giving appreciation is what it does to you. If you're inclined toward Complainer, Cynic, or Controller behaviors, appreciation of others is a very effective path out of your own drama.

CHAPTER 10

THE SEVEN STEPS FOR DEALING WITH DRAMA

In this chapter, we break the successful navigation of drama into two parts: the *dress rehearsal* and the *main act*. The dress rehearsal sets the stage for meeting with the drama-prone person. It includes getting out of your own drama, assessing the types of drama in the other person, and determining the risk of having a direct conversation. The main act is the actual encounter with the person. It includes building rapport, using the tools from chapter 9, getting the person's commitment, and anchoring his new behavior.

The Dress Rehearsal:
Preparing for the Encounter

STEP 1: GET OUT OF YOUR OWN DRAMA

Step 1 starts with you. Before initiating an encounter, you must firmly anchor your own authenticity. If you're frustrated by the antics of a drama-prone person, it's tempting to immediately start using the tools described in chapter 9. You'll want to have the direct conversation, give him an ultimatum, get his agreement, and be done. But as we said in part III, before you can guide others in addressing their drama, you must be authentic and drama-free yourself. Only by keeping your own dramatic behaviors in check can you be present with the other person in a spirit of curiosity while knowing and being ready to cleanly enforce your boundaries.

We've seen far too many managers skip over this stage and get "hooked" by the dramatic behaviors of their colleagues. Their attempts at direct conversations devolve into complaining, blaming, controlling, or rescuing, and the opportunity for collaboration is lost.

STEP 2: DIAGNOSE THE TYPE OF DRAMA
IN THE OTHER PERSON

In this stage, you put together your game plan for approaching the person. Be authentic with yourself and curious about the behaviors of the other person. Then, you can use the diagnostic tools in part II to assess the other person's drama tendencies. Sometimes you'll only be dealing with a single drama type—for example, a pure Complainer. Often, however, a person is prone to fall into multiple dramatic behaviors. It's common to encounter a hybrid drama type like the Controller-Complainer (the Weak King) or the Caretaker-Complainer (the Martyr). Once you know the person's drama type, you can choose the appropriate rapport-building tactics, behavior management approaches, and confrontation tools. See Appendix A for examples.

STEP 3: ASSESS THE RISK OF CONFRONTING THE OTHER PERSON

Before meeting with drama-prone colleagues, you must identify and evaluate the potential downsides of doing so. Without objectively assessing these risks, you might be tempted to either accept a dysfunctional relationship you could have salvaged or make a misstep you could have avoided. So, before launching into a direct conversation with your boss or a team member, consider the possible side effects.

Risk #1. Nothing happens.

No matter what tactics you try, you can't get any traction. The other person just doesn't seem to get it. Your softer, collaborative approaches might yield polite nods and agreements to collaborate, but it's more lip service than real commitment. The progress made is temporary and delays taking more direct action, like delivering an ultimatum.

Risk #2. Resistance increases.

You wake the sleeping bear. The person now resists previous strategies that had been marginally effective. Even though she complained and made excuses, she at least showed up for work and added some value. Now, she displays defensive, retaliatory, or self-righteous behaviors, perhaps putting the issue back on you. Further, she becomes even less predictable in her interactions and assignments.

Risk #3. Chaos erupts.

Not only do you wake the bear, but he goes on a rampage. He starts to drain even more energy with passive-aggressive or other undermining behaviors. He may launch a campaign to rally his peers against you, the bad guy. At their first meeting, Laura was able to prevent pandemonium from erupting, but it was definitely brewing when Theresa and Foster regressed into arguing and finger-pointing.

Risk #4. You push the person too far.

In your efforts to guide a competent person to higher levels, he exceeds his growth or learning limits and actually devolves to a lower level. Your good intentions expose deeper wounds (e.g., low self-esteem, unresolved trauma, family issues, or other emotional baggage) that neither you nor the team is prepared to handle. Fragile Caretakers and Complainers, like Candace and Sam, can have meltdowns if pushed too far.

Risk #5. The relationship ends.

Sometimes the two parties must go their separate ways. This is always a possibility when you candidly address interpersonal tensions or dysfunctional behavior with another person. Even with your careful guidance, the other person might not be ready or willing to let go of his drama. Rather than make the situation worse, the relationship ends.

Be forewarned. There's a side effect to setting clear limits and facing these risks. The longer you've been enabling the inauthentic behaviors of others, the more likely it is that they will blame or vilify you when you start to draw boundaries. They might call you selfish. They might talk about you behind your back. They might not like you anymore. If your sense of self-worth is defined by other people's opinions, you might easily regress into familiar caretaking behaviors. This is where a coach or guide is so important—a friend, coworker, mentor, or family member who can appreciate you for who you are, independent of what you do, and can support you in drawing and maintaining your boundaries.

After your assessment, you might determine that the risks of an encounter are too high. Sometimes, a coworker carries critical information or expertise about a project, client, or strategy that you can't afford to lose. For example, if Laura confronts Theresa, she might become angry and leave the company. Is Theresa's willing collaboration on the Highline project worth the gamble? Would Laura be better off coping with Theresa's cynicism than losing her crucial involvement in other development efforts?

If you decide that a direct confrontation is too chancy, develop coping tactics around the person so that you and your team can at least remain energy-neutral. You might isolate a subordinate as much as possible, gradually pare back his responsibilities, and develop comparable skills in others to avoid being held captive to the "key-man syndrome." The relationship will likely become what we call *transactional*, consisting of well-defined time frames, deliverables, rewards, and penalties. As part of the coping strategy, you should clearly spell out the agreements you make and the ways they will be monitored.

Also remind yourself that you are consciously choosing to accept your colleague's behavior. You might even internally congratulate yourself for making the tough decision. Avoid drifting into your own victimhood by blaming the other person or whining about having to live with her dysfunction. *You* have chosen to accept a draining relationship, and thereby have forfeited your right to complain.

The Main Act:
Meeting with the Drama-Prone Person

You've now addressed your own drama tendencies, determined the likely drama types you'll be dealing with, assessed the risks of confronting the person, and decided you are willing to take the risks. You're now ready for the direct conversation.

STEP 4: DEVELOP RAPPORT WITH THE OTHER PERSON

Before initiating the direct conversation, it's important to establish rapport with the other person so he is best prepared to receive your message. You have one chance to start the meeting off on the right foot, so you need to carefully plan your opening remarks and figure out how you will set the stage for your direct conversation. Your goal is to get the person's full attention and to set him up to be receptive to your ideas.

Your opening remarks will normally be a blend of connection, appreciation, ground rules, and expectations.

Most people prefer to collaborate with colleagues whom they know and like, so strive to establish some shared interests and goals, whether inside or outside of work. These might include family dynamics (you both have teenagers), common backgrounds (both are eldest children, grew up in the same part of the country, similar major in college), or hobbies (sports, music, the arts, church). While you might be frustrated by the drama-prone person's behavior at work, set aside your judgments about the person ("He's such a whiner [know-it-all, bully, weakling]"), and find something to like about him.

Use appreciation at the beginning of the conversation to recognize the other person's gifts, accomplishments, or potential. Remember to be specific and sincere. At least for a moment, filter out your judgments on his drama and focus on his positive attributes. You'll soon be confronting the person on his behaviors, but, initially, a spoonful of sugar helps the medicine go down. Additionally, explain the purpose for the encounter. You've determined that this is a risk worth taking, which means you must see something positive as a probable outcome. Make this known.

As part of rapport-building, set the ground rules for the meeting. This typically includes the expected duration of the meeting, the desire for candid dialogue, and the need for a climate of curiosity and openness. Be clear about what you want from the meeting. Normally this will be a clear agreement about go-forward protocol and behavior in the person's interactions with you and others. You expect him to see beyond his specific wants and complaints and embrace an expanded view.

The following table provides specific rapport-building techniques for the different drama types. In chapter 11 we'll see how Laura models these different forms of rapport-building in her one-on-one meetings with the Highline team members.

HOW TO BUILD RAPPORT WITH THE FOUR DRAMA TYPES	
COMPLAINER	Put yourself in their shoes and acknowledge their experience. You don't have to agree with them; just acknowledge by saying something like, "I can see where you're coming from."
	Complainers usually crave appreciation. Tell them what you value about their contribution. Offer reassurance about your confidence in them and in their capacity to develop.
CYNIC	Show interest in and curiosity about their areas of expertise. Praise their novel thinking. Invite them to be your teacher.
	Express your confidence in their abilities and invite them to share their wisdom and experience with the rest of the team. Honor them for welcoming the ideas of others.
CONTROLLER	Honor their initiative and their desire to "do the right thing."
	Praise any acts of delegation or empowerment you have witnessed or experienced directly.
CARETAKER	Commend them for completing projects in a timely manner, making tough decisions, or drawing boundaries.
	Caretakers feel most connected when they are pleasing others, so let them connect with you or praise you. Graciously receive their appreciation. Then, state how much you appreciate them when they set boundaries and make tough decisions.

STEP 5: USE THE DIRECT-CONVERSATION TOOLS

After you've established a connection with the drama-prone person and have his attention, you can choose the appropriate tools from chapter 9 for defusing the drama. Most exchanges start with the direct-conversation model, leading into either an ultimatum or a clear agreement about behavior and expectations going forward. Anticipate that emotion might arise at any time and you'll have to set aside any attempts at rational discussion. Use the knowledge you have from the discussion on handling emotion in chapter 9 to honor and reflect the emotion until it subsides. Then, you can continue with the direct conversation and eventually arrive at either a clear agreement or an ultimatum.

STEP 6: GET THEIR COMMITMENT

As part of the direct conversation, you'll express your specific requests for or expectations of the person. A commitment to realize these expectations without excuses, sarcasm, self-pity, or martyrdom is often difficult to obtain from drama-prone people. They'll dance around the expectation or rephrase it in vague terms. These deflection or evasion tactics are a self-protection mechanism that helps the dramatic person avoid both change and accountability.

Don't get hooked. These tactics are grounded in emotion—usually fear of change—so reflect back what you are hearing and then reiterate both your specific expectations and your need for the drama-prone person's commitment to meet them. If he continues to resist or deflect, be prepared to calmly lay out an ultimatum, including specific rewards or consequences.

During this commitment stage, it is imperative that you stay out of your own drama. If you have Caretaker tendencies, you might be prone to reduce your expectations of the person, accept his vague promises, or offer to do the work for him. If you fall into this trap, you miss the chance to delegate. If you have Cynic tendencies, you might be inclined to write the person off as incompetent and miss the chance to help him grow. If you like being the Controller, you might move to ultimatums too quickly and miss the chance to empower the individual. And if you're a Complainer, you might be inclined to commiserate, find somebody else to blame, or become a victim yourself, thus denying your responsibility for creating the dynamic.

The Commitment stage demands clarity, creativity, and courage, and it requires that you have already worked through your own drama tendencies. Once you have atttained this self-awareness, you can then remain grounded in mature behaviors when the other person makes his last ditch efforts to cling to his drama.

STEP 7: VALIDATE AND ANCHOR THEIR COMMITMENT AND NEW BEHAVIOR

The main act of the encounter started with connection and appreciation, and it should end in the same way. Praise the person for his positive behaviors during your meeting, and honor the commitments he made. Follow up with a short note or e-mail confirming and affirming the person's commitment and your agreement. Ideally, you'll have such individuals capture their agreements in writing, creating a summary of your meeting that includes their specific commitments. People live up to what *they* write down.

If the person appears demoralized by the end of the meeting, affirm your confidence in his capacity to honor his commitments, including specific appreciation for his committed behavior. However, avoid the tendency to dilute the commitment the person has made or soften your expectations. Stay calm, open, compassionate—and firm.

To help you prepare for an encounter with a drama-prone associate, go to **www.DramaFreeOffice.com** to download a free checklist of the seven-step process.

CHAPTER 11

PUTTING THE TOOLS AND PROCESSES TO WORK

You've released your own drama, diagnosed the drama tendencies of your associate, assessed the risks of a confrontation, and now you're ready for the Big Meeting. You've practiced the different tools and understand the seven-step process. Regardless of how much you've prepared, anticipate that you'll have to deviate from the script. You've read the sheet music; get ready to play jazz.

The best preparation is to get your head in the right place. Regardless of the drama type you'll be confronting, commit to be unattached from the person's behaviors. It is imperative that you stay curious and compassionate, while knowing and enforcing your boundaries. Regardless of the outcome, your most important objective is to stay clear, grounded, and out of your own drama while navigating through the other person's drama.

The rest of this chapter captures Laura's individual meetings with the members of the Highline SWAT team. As you read the narratives, note how she builds rapport with each person and then uses a blend of the different tools (direct conversations, ultimatums, reflecting emotion, clear agreements, and appreciation) to guide him or her out of drama. At the conclusion of each exchange, notice how she anchors the person's go-forward commitment to authentic interactions with the rest of the team.

Assume that Laura has already navigated out of her own drama tendencies (e.g., wanting to disband the team and run the whole project herself) and released her judgments (e.g., chastising Sam for being a whiner and stereotyping Foster as the windbag accountant) prior to each exchange. Also assume that she has previously assessed the risks of confronting each team member (e.g., Theresa leaving the team or Candace having a meltdown), and chose to take these risks. She determined that if deeper issues existed within the individual team members, it was better to surface them now in a one-on-one meeting, even if it meant the person had to leave the group, than to suffer through unproductive, drama-laden team meetings. Laura thought through the risk that the team members might go behind her back to Cliff if she stayed firm on the behavior she expected from them. She was ready to take all of these risks.

So here we go. Showtime. Curtain up on the first act: Laura and Sam—the Complainer.

One-on-One with a Complainer: Laura and Sam

At 12:05 p.m., Sam entered the conference room. Laura was ready.

"Hi, Sam. Come on in. Have a seat." Laura got right to the point. "So what's your reaction to our meeting earlier today?"

"Boy, this is a real mess," Sam said. "I don't see any way out of it. As I said this morning, my team and I have done everything we can to smooth things over with Peter's people, but nothing seems to be working. If we just had a little more time and a few more resources . . . but then Foster talks about cost-cutting and shareholder value, so I guess that will never happen. My department is already stretched. I just don't have an answer."

"I can see you feel you've done everything you can with your existing resources, and you feel your people are pretty stretched," Laura reflected back. "And, at least for right now, there doesn't appear to be any clear solution. Is there anything else coming up for you?"

"Well, between you and me, if we lose Peter's account, I've got virtually no chance of making my targets for the quarter. We'll lose a lot of credibility in the market and Cliff will be all over me to up our sales pace. So, it's a double whammy.

"Plus, I've got a few fragile people behind quota already. They could leave, and I've already got three open positions. I just don't know what could happen. It's a little scary, and frankly, it makes me mad."

"It makes sense to me that you'd feel disturbed about this, and even a little angry," said Laura. "You're worried that you might miss your targets, that future sales will be harder, and that you might even lose a few of your people."

"Yeah, that's it," Sam replied. "But what can I do? You know, I had a similar situation a year ago with a prospect we were about to lose to a competitor. Fortunately, Candace was very helpful then, and, well, maybe she could—"

"Yes, it's a difficult situation," Laura interrupted. "And although using Candace's team is an option, you and I need to get clear on a few things first." She then moved into the direct conversation.

"Sam, the fact is, we have three days as a team to prepare feasible options and present a recommendation to Cliff. In this morning's meeting, you described the situation as a nightmare and a melt-down, while defending your entertainment budget and open hires. In my opinion—and it's only my opinion—you and the other team members were stuck in your own departments' dynamics and strug-gled to see the bigger picture. I need a team committed to thinking collaboratively and to preparing a creative plan for Cliff."

Laura didn't give him a chance to interject. "Part of me is excited about the opportunity to both fix an urgent customer problem and break down some barriers I think exist between departments here at Riva. At the same time, I'm also a little scared we can't really pull it off. It makes me angry when I witness the squabbling among some of the top managers who've been assigned to me to address this problem.

"As you know, I'll be talking with the other team members later this afternoon. Sam, I specifically want you to set aside—at least for the next two days—the possible short-term impact on you and the Sales department and brainstorm new, perhaps out-of-the-box, approaches with Foster, Theresa, Candace, and me. That means showing up with an open, curious mind and putting yourself in the shoes of the others in the room. Is this something you're willing to do?"

Sam blurted out, "Of course I'm willing, but you saw what hap-pened this morning. Theresa will just sabotage my ideas, Candace will promise the world and then under-deliver, and Foster will jockey to take charge of the whole project. Sure, I'll try, but I just don't think there's much I can do."

Laura resisted the urge to throttle him for his whining and reflected back again. "Sam, I understand that you think it will be tough and that you're concerned other people on the team might sabotage the process. I can see how you might feel that way. Is there any more?"

"No, it seems like you get it."

"Sam, I do understand your position—except for one thing. What is it that you really want?" Laura asked.

"Well, what I really want is a reliable product to sell, and for Theresa and Foster to get off my back and let me do my job."

"I understand that you want the freedom you need to do a good job," Laura reflected. Now, the key question: "And if you had that, what is it you really want for yourself?"

Sam sighed. "You know, I would like some respect for the job I do in Sales. We bust our butts, make the numbers, and the bar just moves higher. For once, I'd love to hear a 'great job' from some of the other senior leaders in this company."

Seeing her opening, Laura confirmed his statement. "I get that you want some appreciation—to feel valued—by others in the company. That makes sense to me." With Sam's core want on the table, Laura moved to align it with the big-picture goals of the group.

"Sam, I believe that every person in the room this morning wants to feel valued for his or her contribution at Riva. I know I want this. Yet we all just seem to get caught up in ourselves and lose track of the bigger goal that requires mutual respect and a collaborative frame of mind. We need the company goal to take precedence over our personal frustrations or agendas. Does that make sense?"

"Yeah, Laura. I guess you're right. I can see how we've got to get along."

"Thanks, Sam. Challenges like this project require everyone pulling in the same direction. So when we meet tomorrow morning, can I count on you to take the big-picture view and catch yourself when you begin to defend Sales and start to blame others—at least while we're working through this project?"

"I suppose I can do that."

Sensing Sam's reluctance, Laura pushed for something more definitive. "Then I have a commitment that you'll bring your best ideas to the table tomorrow and stay open to everyone's ideas?"

"Yes, I will do that," he replied.

"Sam, I appreciate you sharing your concerns today, and especially your commitment to brainstorming options with the team tomorrow. This really makes my job easier, and I'm grateful. See you in the morning!"

One-on-One with a Complainer: A Real-Life Example

John was the managing director at a large law firm. The firm was in a period of reorganization meant to lay the organizational foundation for aggressive expansion goals. John was at his wits' end, overwhelmed with too much responsibility. To give him the leverage he needed to perform, he was bringing in a new president, to whom Robert, one of his subordinates, would now report.

Robert had been one of the first associates at the now substantial law firm. But he still hadn't made partner. His clients loved him, he brought in repeat business, and he performed well on the metrics of the job. But he was intolerable to manage. He refused to teach the next layer of young associates his techniques. "It's my secret sauce," he'd say. He felt entitled to everything ("I deserve it!" was his mantra), and he openly commented (to all who would listen) on how hard he worked while not making partner. "No one's there for you," he'd warn new associates. "I've worked so hard, only to have the company take me for granted."

Robert brought the topic of partnership up with John (his boss and the managing partner) on an almost weekly basis. "Why aren't I partner? Look at everything I do. Look at my billable hours." When John mentioned the inappropriateness of talking with junior associates about partnership discussions, Robert just shrugged. When John asked Robert about contributing to the development of the people in the firm, Robert resorted to his all-too-familiar complaining. "I can't. I don't have time. My clients need me, and I'm servicing them. Most of these kids won't stay for the long run anyway . . ." And on and on.

When we met with Robert the first time, he was entrenched in his victim stance. John was subjecting him to training he didn't have time for. It wasn't his fault that the "kids" in the office couldn't pick up the tricks of the trade. If they were smart enough, they'd figure it out on their own.

Our first step was to build rapport with him, so we invested time in sincerely appreciating his skills. He was a masterful attorney. His clients loved him. He did bill a lot of hours. We then reviewed the responsibilities of a partner—primarily his responsibility for maintaining a collaborative culture and investing in the growth of the firm. In the direct conversation, Robert was able to see how he craved appreciation from John, but that his behaviors were getting him the opposite results. He also began to see his contributions in the context of the damage he caused to morale when he complained. We made an agreement that in addition to his continued client performance, Robert would mentor three recent hires personally. He would have a one-on-one meeting with John to review his progress and make a clear agreement on the unambiguous criteria required to make partner. We expressed confidence that Robert could meet these criteria and become a partner. Using a "soft" ultimatum, we also told him that, although the firm would hate to lose him, complaining in the office would be an indicator that it was time for him to move on.

Complainer Epilogue

Complainers, like Sam and Robert, present a tough managerial challenge. Too much rapport-building will launch them into side eddies of complaining, making it difficult to bring them back to the issue at hand. Not enough empathy will have them see you as just another "villain" who doesn't understand them.

When confronted with problems, Complainers can bounce among helplessness, indecision, and deflection. If Laura is too soft, she risks becoming enmeshed in Sam's victimhood. If she's too harsh, she might drive him to consent in the moment, only to have him return to his whining act later.

Laura appropriately chose to forego small talk and immediately sought Sam's opinion on the meeting. She built rapport by reflecting back Sam's story and validating his feelings and views without ever actually agreeing with him. Once they'd connected, she initiated the direct conversation, and after a couple of iterations and more rapport-building, she obtained his commitment to collaborate at the team meeting. She then anchored that commitment with a specific appreciation of both his concerns and his commitment to brainstorm.

One-on-One with a Cynic: Laura and Theresa

"Hi, Theresa. Quite the first meeting with our team, huh? What's your reaction to the session this morning?" asked Laura.

"I saw this coming six months ago, but no one was listening. If I'd been allowed to continue the cutting-edge development project I launched last fall, we wouldn't be in this mess. It's exactly what Peter would have wanted. But instead, we killed the project so we could once again bail out the Sales team. After all, 'gotta make the numbers.' But whatever. You're the project head. Just tell me what you want me to do, and I'll have my team patch together some kind of fix."

Laura took a deep breath and reflected back what Theresa had said. "I hear you saying that you were aware of problems as long as six months ago. And it also sounds like you're carrying some resentment about your development project being canceled."

Anticipating that further rapport-building attempts would be unproductive, Laura took a more direct route. "Theresa, the facts are, you spent most of this morning's meeting with your arms crossed, looking out of the window. You made a handful of remarks about a 'Mayday call from Sales,' 'dodging the bullet,' 'and covering up for lukewarm product testing.' I felt offended by these and can imagine that others felt the same. In my opinion, your comments, body language, and tone of voice distracted us from our goal of brainstorming new options for solving this problem."

Theresa sat upright, her mind whirring with rebuttals. Laura had her attention.

Before Theresa could reply, Laura continued, "Theresa, you are a gifted developer with a great capacity for seeing the big picture and understanding subtleties. You have insights into technologies that neither I nor anyone else on our team has. You have the potential to inject the innovation we need into the Highline project. I'm afraid, though, that you will continue to rehash the past and make judgments about the skills or motives of others rather than channeling your talents into new initiatives. I believe that if you choose this approach, we all lose.

"When we're meeting as a team, I expect you to express interest—and, ideally, curiosity—in others' ideas, while proactively offering your own insights and options about strategies and actions. There will certainly be times for examining and critiquing our plans, and your critical views will be very valuable at that point. However, in other interactions, especially when we're dealing with tough problems or sensitive relationships, I expect your full-out, enthusiastic participation. I ask you to set aside any disagreements you might have with others on the team—or with the company as a whole—and collaborate on a plan we can present to Cliff. We'll discuss and haggle tomorrow. But when we come out of that room, I ask you to commit to this plan, 100 percent, both on the Highline team and back in your own department."

Laura went for the close. "So, Theresa, will you do this?"

Quick to recover, Theresa's Cynic defense mechanisms started to kick in. "I'm *always* the company player. I bail out Sam all the time and live within Foster's ridiculously low budget for R&D. We never learn from our mistakes at this company. We cancel key projects just when they're getting traction. Everything is a crisis. There's no investment in the future. And—"

"Theresa, I get that you see yourself as a company player and that we must learn from the past. You feel we cancel projects too soon, give up the future for the present, and treat everything as urgent. I get that . . . but, Theresa, what is it you really want for yourself?"

This time, Theresa paused and sincerely pondered the question.

"I don't know . . . how about a little respect for the years I've invested here? Maybe some acknowledgement that I really *do* know what I'm talking about. That my ideas are valued. But that'll never happen."

Laura had her opening. "Theresa, it makes total sense that you'd want to be acknowledged for both your tenure here at Riva and your technical contributions. I've checked in with some of the other product managers, and they tell me you are one of the most innovative people in the company."

Theresa looked at Laura. "Really?"

"Really."

Softening, Theresa added, "The last couple of years have been particularly rough. I'm supposed to manage a team, and I get frustrated when we under-design products and miss deadlines. I always made my deadlines in the past. And I get frustrated by the other managers when they don't understand the technology. Sometimes they just don't get it."

Laura saw a rapport-building opportunity. "I can empathize with the shift from developer to manager; I felt the same way several years ago when I took on my first supervisory role. It's tough, especially when we judge that others can't do things as well or as quickly as we can. I appreciate you telling me this. It makes sense to me."

Laura went on, "We have an important meeting tomorrow. We all need to bring our A-game to the table. Now, more than ever, we need your creative thinking. And the same from Sam, Foster,

Candace, and me. This can only happen if we're all willing to set aside our judgments and grievances—anything we're carrying from the past—and focus collaboratively on great solutions for Highline.

"There's one other thing: To optimize our time tomorrow, we all need to let go of our need to be right. There are no mistakes. You never know—what seems like a bogus or dumb idea, when massaged a little bit, could turn out to be exactly what we need. So, I ask you to trust the process tomorrow. If we respect and support one another, I have a hunch something great could happen."

Laura paused for a moment. "Are you in?"

"I'll give it a shot."

"So, do I have your commitment to bring an open, curious mind and your best ideas to the table tomorrow?"

"Yes, you do," Theresa said.

One-on-One with a Cynic: A Real-Life Example

Elise was an emergency room doctor at a large metropolitan hospital. She and her colleagues working the midnight shift witnessed the most gruesome accidents night after night. She was an efficient, "all business" doctor who saved the lives of those in trauma, but she was toxic as a colleague. The team of nurses and other doctors knew that Elise was smart and had worked in several other institutions, so they hoped she would bring valuable best practices to the hospital. But she didn't seem willing.

In the hospital meetings where doctors, nurses, and administrators gathered to share best practices, discuss policy changes, and address institutional issues, Elise was known to sit in the back with her arms crossed. She didn't want to be in most meetings—and she made it obvious. "*Talking* about medicine is a waste of time! And teambuilding exercises are pointless," she would say. "I'm an ER doctor, and I'd rather be out *doing* my *real* job. Policies and staff both change like the wind, so why even bother?" Once, a colleague, trying to be thoughtful, said, "Are you alright? You look a little tired." Elise retorted, "Well you look fat, so I guess we both look bad."

Elise was a stickler for perfection, reminding people that their focused efforts often meant the difference between life and death. Mistakes were intolerable and seamless transitions between teams were mandatory. Yet, as she evaluated everyone around her, she was perpetually negative. Nurses didn't know enough, patients were crybabies, and the other doctors sat around in meetings discussing policies rather than working. She was known to make comments like, "Gang members kill each other, no matter how much education we do. Obese people will continue to eat fast food until the heart attack kills them. Health care will never be fixed, so why bother trying?" Her pessimistic view of everyone and everything was polluting the hospital environment.

When we came in to work with the ER team, Elise was struck by the description of a Cynic. She recognized herself immediately. Yet she also felt stuck. "Some things really are a waste of time and energy," she said, defending herself. "If you look at health care in this country, we've been working on it with limited success for decades."

We learned that she had once been an advocate for new ideas and change, but had grown frustrated by the lack of progress she had seen, and so had retreated into cynicism. Elise had lost hope that the inefficiencies in the system would ever change. She had given up on patients who refused to make the simple lifestyle changes that would save their lives. She hated team meetings because they felt like a rehash of all the ideas she had seen fail in previous situations.

When Elise realized that her cynical behavior was contributing to the problems that irritated her, she became willing to try again. We encouraged her to focus her efforts on a few simple things that she believed still could change.

Now, after reevaluating her attitude, Elise is on only one task force, the one that reads all grant proposals for the hospital. She uses her quick mind and ability to see what is missing to identify the small changes that can make a big difference to patients' health. She sees this as a way to help improve her colleagues' suggestions and make good policy decisions without getting mired in areas that she knows induce disparaging comments. While it is unlikely that she will ever be a hallway cheerleader, Elise has been able to limit her cynical behavior to just a single joke or sarcastic comment and shift back to a constructive observation about something that can be changed for the better. She also catches herself when she starts to become negative about situations outside of her control, like hospital policies or the health care system. She acknowledges her frustration about the situation and then refocuses on the areas she can affect—like delivering stellar care to her ER patients.

Cynic Epilogue

Debating with Cynics like Theresa and Elise can be frustrating, and it's often futile. Laura chose the direct route early in her conversation, quickly getting to her big wants: releasing the past, focusing on the present problem, and collaborating as a team.

When Theresa fell back into excuses, blaming, and rhetoric, Laura used the cut-to-the-core question, "What do you really want for yourself?" The Cynic will often deflect this question, sharing wants related to the team or other individuals (e.g., "I want Foster to relax the budgets"). You might need a couple of iterations, but keep asking the question until you get a meaningful, personal desire from the Cynic. Frequently, it will have something to do with being respected, valued, or appreciated. Then, as Laura did, you can tie this in to the ultimate goal of the team.

Most Cynics long to be recognized for their innate abilities—in Theresa's case, her innovation skills. After sincerely praising her for these, Laura invited her associate to channel them into team-level collaboration. She then got Theresa's commitment to bring an open, curious mind to the discussions. Notice that this took two rounds. Theresa's first response—"I'll give it a shot"—was lukewarm. With all drama types, make sure you get a clear "Yes, I will" affirmation when you ask for a commitment or make an agreement.

One-on-One with a Controller: Laura and Foster

"Hey, Foster. Glad you could make it. Let's get down to business: What was your reaction to the meeting this morning?"

This was the only opening Foster needed. "If you really want to know . . . I'm furious! I know it's your project, but I can't believe you let those incompetents and whiners hijack the meeting. Laura, the best thing is for you and me to sit down for a couple of hours and come up with a plan. I saw this type of crisis a dozen times at my old job. This is exactly the problem I came to Riva to solve. I'm surprised Cliff didn't put me in charge, but no matter—you say the word and I'll get it fixed. The company needs you focused on Operations. I'm happy to take this off your plate."

Sensing her heart rate rise, Laura thought, *This should be interesting*. She took a deep breath and made her first move. "I can see you're upset about the meeting this morning. I hear you've witnessed this type of crisis multiple times in your old job, and you'd really like to run the Highline project yourself. I appreciate your drive. The project needs it."

Foster nodded vigorously.

"However," Laura continued, "your comments about whiners, incompetence, and hijacking cause me to question your commitment to me, the team, and even the company. In my judgment, this project requires the seamless collaboration of the four disciplines represented by the team members: sales, technology, customer service, and your expertise, finance. Each manager brings skills in certain areas and inexperience in others. We must pool everyone's talents. Your resourcefulness is admirable; we absolutely need you on the team. And I even appreciate your desire to run the project. But I have been charged to lead this project—and I will do so.

"I—we all—need your initiative and drive," Laura continued. "You're dedicated to having things done right. I saw that when you overhauled our financial systems and got our cash flow back in line. Now, we need that same attention to detail and deadline management aligned with the team's objectives. Can I count on you for this?"

Foster paused for a moment. Red in the face and measuring his words, he replied, "All right, just tell me what you want me to do."

Laura had a tough decision. Part of her wanted to pitch him on being a collaborative "good boy" at tomorrow's meeting and end the discomfort of this encounter. But she also sensed that he was stewing in emotion, and, if left unaddressed, his stuffed frustration would leak out later, most likely during tomorrow's meeting. It was risky, but allowing him to vent might lead to a breakthrough. She decided to go for it.

"Foster, I notice that you're a little flushed and that you're choosing your words carefully. It looks like you've got something on your mind."

He erupted. He went into his failing to make partner at his prior job, his string of incompetent bosses, his struggles to make an impression on Cliff, and a stream of other buried frustrations. Staying detached, Laura listened, rephrased, reflected back his comments, and occasionally asked, "Is there more?" She was careful not to offer advice or judgment.

After a while, he became quiet and stood up to leave. That's when Laura asked the breakthrough question. "Foster, what is it that you really want for yourself?"

He sat back down, sighed, and said, "I just want to be respected for my work and to have something I can call my own. I really want to be trusted to run something. I want people to believe in me."

Laura looked him in the eye and said, "Foster, I really get it that you want to be respected, to have others believe in you, and to have something you can call your own. It makes total sense to me that you would want this. My commitment to you is that I will find some piece of this project—not the whole thing—that can be yours to run. But there's a condition. In return, I need your commitment to listen to, collaborate with, and support every person on this team—Sam, Theresa, Candace, and me—regardless of our experience or role. In other words, show the same respect for us that you seek for yourself."

"Okay, Laura, I'm willing to do that."

"I also have a suggestion for you. Are you open to it?"

"Sure, what is it?" he asked.

"Again, it's just a suggestion, but give it some thought. For you to really blossom professionally, let go of the need to run this project—or, for that matter, to run anything. Consider that real leadership is determined by your ability to empower others. If we both do this, I believe our careers will flourish."

He nodded.

"Foster, thanks for this time today. I appreciate your candor with me. And I believe in you. See you in the morning."

One-on-One with a Controller: A Real-Life Example

If he didn't bring in such great numbers, David would have been fired a year ago. He was the primary business development person at a remote office of a product development company. His job was to craft engaging proposals and then close deals with large companies. And he was very good at this. But as his deals neared closure, chaos reigned in his small office. His team walked on eggshells around him and avoided interaction as much as possible. They admitted to being afraid of him. His expectations were impossible to meet—as shown by the criticism he had for everything that crossed his desk. None of their work was ever good enough for him, and he often reduced his team members to tears. If there was a mistake, he would berate the person mercilessly—and it was an open office. The team members told us it felt like they were working under a tyrant.

Meanwhile, David thought the headquarters team was a joke—it didn't deliver the numbers he did. So, he gave himself full rein to do whatever he wanted and treat his satellite office like his own fiefdom.

David's boss was aware of the staff's unrest and had approached David, suggesting that he consider the impact of his perfectionism on his associates. But David reacted with anger, and his boss backed off. After all, David's production was great; why rock the boat? Due to his tenure at the company and deal-making genius, no one, not even his boss, had the courage to confront him.

The team needed outside help and sought our counsel. Once we discerned the situation, we knew we had a Controller on our hands and provided the necessary tools to both David's team and his boss. The team embraced the direct-conversation model. It gave the team members a structure both sides could follow when clearing the air on an issue.

We also invested time in building a relationship with David, who as you might imagine was suspicious of both our presence and motives. As trust slowly developed, we were able to confront him on his behaviors. At first, as with his boss, he reacted with resentment. We simply listened, reflected back his frustration and anger, and patiently waited for them to pass. We then returned to the direct-conversation model to focus on his behaviors and their impact.

Being able to clearly identify the facts of the situation before discussing any judgments or requests gave David room to listen—a new skill for him. He gradually learned to receive our observations, which helped him expand his perspective. After working with us to brainstorm win-win outcomes for the situation, David made a major shift, expressing his desire to help the company grow and to empower others to do the same. We coached his Caretaker boss on how to bound David's authority—to let him have freedom within his specific sphere of influence, and nothing more.

David continues to push the envelope with his team (it's why he's so successful in his work). The team has embraced reflective listening to dampen the impact of his occasional outbursts. His colleagues also learned to give him options on what is possible, while reminding him of what isn't possible. He and his boss clearly define agreements to minimize surprises and keep everyone on track.

David still has tendencies to regress back to his Controller behaviors. He'll often catch himself raising his voice or taking over a project. It takes consistent feedback from his team, and vigilance on his own part, to stay authentic in his interactions.

The direct-conversation model has become a mainstay in the office. Both the team and David have committed to addressing issues as soon as they arise, ensuring that they don't fester. This work is never done, so the team invests a day off-site every quarter to synchronize priorities, share learning, and address any cultural issues so that the office remains drama-free.

Controller Epilogue

Like Cynics, Controllers respond best to directness, especially when they're in a place of anger, as Foster was. Small talk and rapport-building rarely work under these circumstances. Better to reflect back the anger, and then match the Controller's blunt remarks with straightforward statements. Controllers will attack ambiguity, so after honoring Foster's admirable traits—his resourcefulness and desire to lead—Laura made her own boundaries very clear: "I will lead this project."

She was then precise about the behavior she required from him. Controllers would rather keep assignments vague so they can do what they want. They become annoyed when forced to follow others' explicit directives. Many managers back down at this point, afraid of agitating the Controller further. They make blurry agreements, hoping things turn out for the best. This just pushes the inevitable confrontation into the future and usually leads to ongoing frustration on the part of all parties. Laura used a soft ultimatum: Foster could earn a piece of project leadership only through his commitment to collaborate with and support every person on the team.

Notice how Laura handled Foster's obvious, yet unexpressed, emotion. She could have ignored the signal and missed an opportunity to connect with him. Instead, she acknowledged his telltale body language and simply said, "It looks like you've got something on your mind."

The longer emotion has been buried, the less you can predict how it will be expressed. Many managers panic when emotion arises in their associates, wanting to call in Human Resources or outside therapists at the first sign of tears or an angry outburst. The vast majority of the time, all you need to do is stay present, listen, reflect back what the other person is saying or doing, and occasionally ask, "Is there more?" As with Laura and Foster, the emotion will eventually subside, and you can get to the pivotal question: "What do you really want?" This question is the gateway to collaboration and clear agreements.

One-on-One with a Caretaker:
Laura and Candace

"Come in, Candace. I really appreciate you being available late in the day like this, and I commit to limiting this meeting to twenty minutes at the most. The goal is for both of us to prepare for tomorrow. But before we get started on that, what was your reaction to our meeting this morning?"

"Oh, don't worry about the time, Laura. After this morning, I imagine you've been very busy, and I can stay as long as you want. About the meeting, I felt awful with everyone arguing, particularly when I'm very willing to take on the brunt of the project. After all, it does seem to be mostly a service issue. I can shuffle a few of my people around to work on Highline. Especially since Sam and Theresa have full plates already. Like I said this morning, I can also—"

"Candace, I really appreciate your concern for the company and desire to solve this problem as easily as possible. Thank you. Your willingness to help means a lot to me.

"After the meeting this morning, I did a little checking on some of your recent projects. Although you helped Sam in landing a key account a couple of months ago, the side effects were considerable. Two QA projects with Theresa fell behind schedule significantly, and the extra travel charges you incurred exceeded even our contingency budgets. I also checked with HR. All your people have received stellar reviews from you, but there don't seem to be any internal candidates for your open supervisory slot.

"From this, I can imagine that, while you are a very hard worker and devoted to the company, you are having some difficulty assessing the scope of new problems—both their duration and the skill level they require of the team. You also want to make sure the work is done well, so you do a lot of it yourself. As a result, your people don't seem to have much of a chance to really grow; they don't seem to feel empowered."

Seeing her slumped shoulders and hurt expression, Laura said, "Candace, keep in mind that these are my observations and my judgments. I notice you've slumped some in your chair. What's coming up for you as I share this?"

"I don't know, Laura. I just love fixing problems and seeing people enjoy their work. Sam's people bring in the business we need as a company, and we absolutely must have Theresa's new products for the future . . . I'm the service center for the company. I've got to do everything I can to minimize their problems. Isn't that what I'm supposed to do?"

Laura saw the opportunity for a teaching moment. "Candace, your desire to fix problems and create harmony in the office is admirable. But resources are finite, even yours. When you reassign resources based on urgent projects or problems, someone or something ends up getting shortchanged. Sometimes it's Sam; sometimes, Theresa. Often, it's the quality of work from your department. And you, personally, might be paying the biggest price. As you commit beyond your reserves, your own health and mental sharpness will suffer. And when you're off your game, everybody loses. Can you see how this might happen?"

Candace sighed. "Yeah, I can see that. I know I need to take better care of myself. I just want to be seen as doing a good job for the company."

She had just shared her own core want without Laura having to ask. Now, Laura could link Candace's desire with the goals of the team. "I see that you really want to be seen as doing good work for the company," Laura reflected back. "And in talking with Sam, Theresa, and Foster, I can tell you that we all want that exact same thing—a sense of being respected and valued for our contributions. Unfortunately, we've been using some approaches that generate more drama than results.

"In your case, you produce drama when you commit beyond your capacities, seeking to keep everybody happy. Instead, consider that the best way for you to serve the company, and our project team, is to commit to what you know you can finish and to use your resources creatively.

"Before our meeting tomorrow morning, I'd like you to assess your current workload and your team's capacity. Get clear on your limits. When we start collaborating on strategies and resource needs, I want you to speak up when you feel you'll be too stretched. You may get pushback from the others. Consider their requests, but hold your ground. And if you feel boxed in, say something like, 'Gee, that's a tough one,' and I'll know that's my cue to help you out."

"Thanks, Laura, but I don't want you to have to bail me out tomorrow. I should be able to handle this."

"Candace, experienced managers know when to ask for help. Besides this project's success, I want to see all of us grow as managers while we work together, and asking for help is actually a key part of your own growth. Will you be willing to do that tomorrow?"

"Of course," said Candace. "Wow, I'm really excited about working on this team!"

"That's great!" Laura said. "And it looks like we finished well within the twenty minutes we set aside for this meeting. I look forward to the brainstorming session with you and the team tomorrow."

One-on-One with a Caretaker: A Real-Life Example

Denise was the founding entrepreneur of a venture-backed company in her hometown. As a lifelong resident, she knew everyone both inside and outside of work. People were always asking about how things were going. She was known as a particularly nice person, and everyone liked her. Whenever there was a problem, Denise was the first to chip in, and then go the extra mile. She seemed to forget that she was the founder and was supposed to be focused on strategy. She came to believe that it was her job to make sure that everyone was happy all the time. At one point, she was running every department with the level of detail of a front-line supervisor. As you can imagine, she was running them all poorly, and the entire company suffered.

When she first learned about the Caretaker role, Denise defended her responsibility to take care of everyone. While at first everyone appreciated Denise for always stepping in, when I interviewed her colleagues, they said the investors were on the fence about keeping her in her current role—she just wasn't cutting it as the CEO. Her staff members liked her; they just didn't respect her. The company was struggling to find the right people, to retain good hires, to help people feel engaged and empowered, and to connect people to the vision the company sold its investors.

Everyone in Denise's organization required coaching and attention to break the company-wide Caretaker-Complainer pattern. The organization switched to a model of clear requests. Rather than having problems "floated" for someone to pick up, individuals explicitly asked other individuals to complete projects and tasks. In response, people began to politely, yet firmly, challenge Denise when she made a commitment. She learned to approach her staff after meetings to renegotiate agreements once she realized she was at risk of breaking them. Denise still has to be careful not to hear others' comments as complaints that she could (and should) solve. And she's needed to learn to let others make mistakes and learn from them, rather than doing everything herself. Her team continues to coach her to be a long-term leader rather than a firefighting hero.

Caretaker Epilogue

Managing Caretakers requires a careful balance between affirmation (to keep them engaged) and directness (to help them grow). Laura established a connection with Candace by opening with appreciation and then expressing curiosity about her reactions to the morning meeting. Laura modeled boundary-setting, a key growth area for Caretakers, by limiting her meeting time with Candace. She then let her colleague ramble for a bit before gently taking control.

Caretakers tend to stay in their "everything is going to work out just fine" bubble if they don't get a reality check, so supervisors must present the Caretaker with irrefutable facts verifying the overcommitment or enabling behavior. Otherwise, Caretakers will rationalize actions to either smooth over disagreements or assure they can get the job done. Laura kindly, but directly, brought Candace back to reality with the references to the late QA charges, blown travel budget, and lack of intradepartmental promotions.

Bald accusations will close down a Caretaker and block productive coaching. Notice Laura's softer language like "I *imagine that*" and "your people *don't seem to*." Laura then owned these statements as her own judgments, making it clear that they were not company-wide character indictments of Candace. During the rest of the conversation, Laura sandwiched behavior observations, coaching suggestions, and specific requests between rapport-building affirmations and encouragement.

Notice how Laura also used "we" language in the closing exchange. Unlike most Cynics and Controllers, Caretakers really want to belong to a team—to be accepted. They just go about this in an unproductive way by pleasing, fixing, and enabling. The statement "I want to see *all of us grow* as managers as we *work together . . .*" tells Candace that Laura will support her when she test-drives her boundaries at the group meeting.

Laura has taken the important first step in purging the drama on her team by having the direct conversation with each of the individual team members. Notice the diversity of interaction skills required to guide them out of their respective drama holes. She needed to be firm and blunt with the Cynic and Controller, yet soft and suggesting with the Complainer and Caretaker. She wove in rapport-building and appreciation for all of them, in a form each person could understand and receive. She also struck an agreement with each one to participate collaboratively in the group brainstorming session. And the one ultimatum was presented in the softer form of a condition with Foster.

Laura left for the day—a long and good day—confident about the progress the team would make in tomorrow's meeting.

CHAPTER 12

THE TEAM MEETING

Dramatic behavior in team meetings is more difficult to address in the moment, especially when emotions are running high. We saw this in the initial SWAT meeting: Trust was low, and the four managers were stuck in their own versions of being right. They were beginning to fall into uncontrollable drama, so Laura appropriately ended the meeting, knowing she had to build a connection with them individually to prepare them for productive exchanges as a team.

Having laid this groundwork with each person, Laura can be more forthright in this second team meeting. However, she must still anticipate her own drifts back into judgments about the individual team members, her instinctive need to take charge and give directives, and her innate tendency to rescue. During the meeting, she must keep a sub-process going on inside her head to keep these inclinations in check.

Once the meeting starts, she'll need to remind them about expected behaviors and help them shift back into collaboration if they drift into their familiar sabotaging habits. As you observe the flow of the meeting, look for how she uses the specific drama-defusing tools presented in previous chapters.

The Meeting

Laura walked in cheerily. "Good morning, everyone. How was your evening?" Laura intentionally chose to launch the meeting with some rapport-building in order to test-drive the openness and connection among the team members—especially after yesterday's direct conversations.

A little guarded, yet willing to talk, the five colleagues exchanged pleasantries for a few minutes. Laura then set the stage. "As you know, our job is to present recommendations to Cliff for resolving the Highline crisis. Our goal today is to stretch beyond our personal and departmental interests, brainstorm creative approaches, and then narrow those down to one or two. So everyone's ideas are welcome. If we stay open and curious, my hunch is that some common themes will emerge, along with one or two breakthrough options."

Everyone nodded in agreement.

Laura continued, "If I sense we're getting bogged down or if any of us starts falling into the drama of yesterday morning's meeting, I will pull us back to brainstorming and collaboration. And if you sense I'm getting caught up in drama myself, *please* let me know. Remember our goals: one, reestablish a strong relationship with Peter's company, while—two—sustaining our ongoing sales and development efforts, and—three—always being aware of costs. So the floor is open. What do you see as our options?"

Tentative at first, the team members soon began to voice ideas. Laura acted as scribe, capturing their suggestions on a whiteboard. For a time, the four managers remained respectful of one another, recalling Laura's request to be open, curious, and collaborative. But before too long, they began drifting into their familiar patterns of needing to be right.

When maintenance rebates were proposed, Sam moaned about missing his sales targets. He then fell into a poor-me whirlpool, complaining about tight budgets and attrition within his team.

When the group seemed stumped over where to get the technical resources for rescuing the Highline account, Candace once again offered to save the day by reassigning her entire Quality Assurance team to Peter's company for "just a little while." Ever the heroine, she rationalized that this would protect Theresa's development projects and Sam's presales technical-support efforts.

At first, Theresa offered some novel approaches for handling the Highline triage that could also be leveraged in her new product development. Then, however, she slipped back into her comfortable contrarian role, slouching in her chair and beginning her sentences with "But that won't work because . . . "

Foster piggybacked on everyone's ideas, offering variations of approaches he'd used in his prior positions. But when the team didn't immediately embrace his proposals, his voice rose and he reverted back to hammering on the one area he felt he could control: cost-cutting.

As the meeting started to spiral downward, Laura said, "Okay, let's stop for a moment. Everyone take a couple of deep breaths and notice what's going on.

"Look at the whiteboard. I think we began with a very productive round of brainstorming. You were curious and collaborative, feeding off each other's ideas. Take a moment now and reflect on your own behavior. I'm going to give each of you some feedback, and I invite you to stay open-minded.

"Foster, I notice you spoke again about your extensive experience in other companies, which has high value here. And while cost-cutting is an option, can you be open to others, perhaps by coming up with a hybrid solution that incorporates all our recommendations?"

Foster started to blurt out a quick response, but caught himself. Pausing and recalling his one-on-one meeting with Laura, he replied, "Thanks for the reminder, Laura. Let me think for a bit on some creative options on costs." A little scared, he took a big risk: "I could also look at delaying the open hire in my own department."

Laura smiled warmly. "Thanks, Foster. Whether or not we pursue that, I appreciate your bigger-picture thinking.

"Candace," Laura continued, "once again, your willingness to offer your QA and Customer Service teams for short-term triage is admirable. However, as we discussed yesterday, consider how reassigning your people would have a negative ripple effect on product development and client retention. What's another approach you might take?"

Candace resisted her natural urge to rescue and replied, "It looks like I did it again. This is really tough for me because I really want these projects to go well. But I see how this leads to my becoming overcommitted. I guess I've got a blind spot. I'll need all of you to support me as I set limits on what I can really deliver."

Laura said, "Candace, it takes a lot of guts for you—and I know for me also—to admit to needing support. I'm happy to help you prioritize, and I'll bet the rest of the team will also."

They all smiled and nodded.

Laura then turned toward Theresa and said, "Your thoughts on how we can leverage the Highline repairs with your time-critical development efforts are superb. They could save the company a lot of time and money. But, Theresa, when you start sentences with 'but'—as I just did—it's harder to hear those good ideas. Personally, it pushes me to go on the defensive, and I lose the momentum of the brainstorming. We need you to share the wisdom of your experience, *along with* supporting and refining our suggestions."

As the reflexive "but" began to form in her mind, Theresa caught herself and said, "You know, I'd really like our products to be innovative and work perfectly, so I get frustrated when we have these kind of breakdowns. Thanks for the reminder about my overanalysis and tendency to criticize. I very much want to find a joint solution for Highline."

Encouraged by the positive responses, Laura said to the last manager, "Sam, I can see how maintenance rebates, on their own, might restrict your sales plan and how there's a risk that you'll lose some of your key people. What's another way you might look at this?"

Sam was a quick study. He recalled the suggestions from Laura yesterday afternoon, and he'd seen how the other team members had just now shifted out of their drama and back to being collaborative. "Thanks, Laura," he said. "Like everybody else, I want the Highline situation to be resolved in the right way. I just tend to get stuck in my own department's issues. I'm ready to get back to brainstorming, and at some point, I'd welcome some suggestions on creative ways to hit our sales targets. One thing's for sure: I don't have all the answers."

Laura could sense a distinct, upbeat shift in the room. She had pushed the reset button and they were back on track. "Nice work, everyone. Notice how easy it is for each of us to lose sight of the big picture. I applaud all of us for committing to collaboration. Now, let's take another approach on the brainstorming. Put yourself in Peter's shoes. As CEO of Highline and a longtime friend of Cliff's, what does Peter really want? What is his 'big want'?"

Again, Laura captured ideas, and themes began to emerge. Sam distilled them. "Peter wants three things: one, a working product; two, fair value for his investment; and three, some form of reparation for the screw-ups—more than just saying we're sorry. Oh yes, and maybe a fourth: a restored relationship with Cliff."

These insights elevated the discussion. Laura provided course corrections out of drama a couple of times, but generally stayed in the background as the team moved into a collaborative rhythm. After more brainstorming, the four managers and Laura agreed on the plan shown on the next page. They committed to specific roles, with measurable intermediate milestones and clear timelines.

They decided that Sam would continue to personally manage the relationships with key Highline personnel, as well as substantially reduce entertainment expenses until Highline was fully satisfied. Theresa would champion the product-stabilization stage, directing a hybrid team of Sales, Technical Support engineers, and one of Candace's QA specialists. Theresa would also lead the performance-enhancement and new-functionality efforts, leveraging the expertise of her developers. Candace would be available for advice, but would have no other explicit involvement with the Highline situation. Instead, she'd focus on backlogged QA efforts, which were delaying the release of another Riva product.

In an unexpected move, Foster agreed to support Sam's new hires and to delay hiring someone for his open Senior Accountant position. In return, the team chose Foster as the operating lead on the entire project, with Laura being the liaison to Cliff.

Laura beamed as she saw the team taking responsibility for both the project and their respective roles. Candor, curiosity, and mutual empowerment and appreciation had replaced the complaining, concealing, defensiveness, and caretaking she had witnessed the day before. *This is really going to work*, she thought. *Now, how do I approach Cliff?*

**THE HIGHLINE TEAM'S RECOMMENDATION:
A STAGED SOLUTION**

1. Create a tailored, working product for Highline, with a concerted blitz effort on all open bugs.

2. Focus on a second, customized release for Highline with the desired performance enhancements.

3. Once the base product required by Highline is working well, add the new functionality.

During these first three stages, waive all maintenance fees to Highline (addresses Peter's "fair value" and "reparation" needs).

Epilogue

Energy-draining drama can surface in any meeting, especially when participants are addressing difficult cross-company problems. The best antidote is prevention, as Laura showed by holding the one-on-one discussions the day before the meeting. But we saw that even with her preparation, sabotaging behaviors can easily hijack a meeting.

When drama does arise in a meeting, a leader must quickly evaluate the risk of addressing it in public. Before Laura's first meeting with her team, she had neither assessed the depth of her associates' drama nor established a sufficient rapport with them to confront them directly at that time. When you sense that emotional undercurrents and the need to be right are overriding curiosity and openness, follow Laura's lead: Adjourn the meeting and schedule one-on-one coaching time with the drama-prone team members. Commit to having the difficult conversations.

When a more aware group—like the Highline team after having direct conversations with Laura—drifts into drama, you can normally shift group members out of it during the meeting and return to collaboration. The same tactics that apply for self-shifting can be used in a meeting when collaboration goes awry and the group starts to drift into drama. The table below shows how the meeting leader can shift the entire group out of drama.

HOW TO SHIFT OUT OF DRAMA DURING A MEETING

- Stop and take a breath.
- Invite drama-prone participants to acknowledge their drift into drama.
- Encourage each person to take responsibility for the negative dynamic in the meeting.
- Recommit to being curious.
- Grant an "absolute pardon" for the drift—forgive and move on.
- Start collaborating!

Now that you've seen Laura run a successful brainstorming session, you might be eager to try it yourself. Before we move on, here are a few tips that will help you stifle drama and build authenticity as your team brainstorms.

TIPS FOR RUNNING A BRAINSTORMING SESSION

- Solicit, praise, and reinforce curiosity and creativity.
- Seek everyone's input.
- Designate a scribe for capturing everything—without judgments.
- Look for patterns, themes, and piggybacking.
- Keep asking, "What if . . ."
- Use the group to consolidate and cull options.
- Set a time limit.
- Conclude with a round of appreciation.

Dealing with the four drama types during meetings is an ongoing challenge. Use the tools in this chapter to eliminate drama from your meetings, and refer to our website (**www.DramaFreeOffice.com**) for even more ways to create a drama-free work environment.

CHAPTER 13

MANAGING UP

Perhaps the most important person you manage in the workplace is your boss. Unfortunately, most subordinates tend to fall into a victimhood posture, believing they have no influence over their boss's behavior and that they can only react. As Laura has shown, you have better options.

"Managing up" requires that you do your homework on your boss's values and attitudes, what she best responds to, and her capacity to be curious and receive feedback. Your job is then to craft your "upward management" style to match her personality and ability to listen. Remember that this decision on communication style is always your conscious choice.

Directing a boss caught in drama requires both calmness and alertness. You have little chance of influencing her behavior if you're caught up in your own dramatic behaviors. Emotional displays, arguing, or rationalizing might feel good, but such behaviors rarely lead to clear agreements.

You can't change anyone's personality, least of all your boss's. However, you can be clear on your own boundaries in the relationship. It's important to know where you are on the following job-flexibility spectrum:

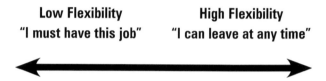

Low Flexibility   **High Flexibility**
"I must have this job"   **"I can leave at any time"**

If you are more to the left on this spectrum, you'll likely forego direct conversations with your superiors, instead choosing to seek clear agreements and accepting that the relationship will be more transactional than authentic. You might enlist other advisors or coaches to brainstorm coping tactics and offer support (*not* a pity party), or to maintain your own authenticity. If you are to the left on this spectrum, be wary of the tendency to fall into the helpless victimhood of the Complainer. Though the consequences might be serious (e.g., getting fired and not being able to pay your mortgage), you still have the choice to leave. So, acknowledge that you are still *choosing* to work in the drama-laden environment. No one is forcing you to stay. You are consciously accepting your current situation, including your boss's behavior, and you forfeit your right to complain. While this might sound insensitive, it captures the reality of accepting full responsibility for your life. It's also the gateway out of being a Complainer.

As with coaching subordinates or peers, successfully coaching your boss requires your own maturity and authentic approach to relationships. You have little chance of influencing your boss's behavior if you are caught up in your own drama. Feeling cynical or sorry for yourself might feel good or "right," but it won't change your situation. If you acknowledge and accept your own healthy responsibility for being in a difficult dynamic with your boss, you increase your odds of shifting the dynamic.

Lacking any authority over your boss, your goal is at best an energy-enhancing relationship and at worst an energy-neutral one. As with subordinates, it is important to preemptively assess the risk of having an encounter with your boss. You might accomplish nothing more than being labeled a malcontent. You might trigger her dormant hostility and experience backlash or passive-aggressive behavior. You could be either ostracized or have a ceiling placed on your career growth, at least in your current organization. And you might get fired. None of these are a certainty, but you should at least assess their probability.

If you choose to approach your boss, stay positive and envision a collaborative relationship. Find things you like about her, no matter how difficult that might seem. Set aside your biases and focus on her strong points. And, above all, you need to commit to your own authenticity. Healthy responsibility and authenticity are contagious—help your boss catch them both.

Specific tactics for managing each of the four different drama roles in your boss were presented in part II. On the following pages are general tips for working with a boss caught in drama, no matter what type of dramatic tendencies she shows.

GENERAL TIPS FOR WORKING WITH A DRAMATIC BOSS

1	Show your support for him, especially in difficult situations or during challenging times. Let your boss know "you have his back."
2	Always bring in a positive attitude. Stay calm, upbeat, and interested.
3	Come prepared with a suite of options and your recommendations any time you bring a problem. Then, be open to feedback from your boss, including both new options and options you had rejected. Stay curious!
4	Show your thinking, including the options you dismissed and the rationale for your recommendations.
5	Put yourself in your boss's shoes. Anticipate the issues your boss is facing with *his* boss or board. Connect your reasoning to the big picture.
6	When he falls into drama, reflect back your boss's emotions and honor his perspective while staying unattached. Never negotiate or rationalize with a boss caught in emotion.
7	Take care of yourself. Gently, yet firmly, ask for what you want related to career growth or compensation. Ideally, provide a suite of options acceptable to you, and ask for his commitment to support you.
8	Be tenacious about requiring clear, measurable, written agreements on your job requirements. If your boss insists on keeping assignments vague or ambiguous, maintain a paper trail of all meetings or communication related to your efforts.

| 9 | Avoid pity parties or gossip groups with your colleagues, especially where they or you are complaining about your boss. If you must vent, do so with dispassionate third parties who have no connection to or vested interest in your organization. |
| 10 | Commit to finding fulfillment, whether it's in your work or in hobbies outside of work. If you are unable to develop an authentic relationship with your boss, you might need to focus on the latter option. |

Laura's Meeting with Cliff

Laura has guided the four team members out of their individual dramas and laid the groundwork for collaborative interactions. She got each of them to agree on a recommended course of action, but she now has one more potentially drama-filled interaction before work can begin—her conversation with Cliff, the boss.

Late Tuesday afternoon, Laura let Cliff know that she and her team had come up with a workable solution to the crisis. She arranged to meet with him the next morning—two days ahead of schedule. On Tuesday evening, she prepared for the meeting.

We learned in the first chapter that Cliff was charismatic, gregarious, and ambitious. These traits, along with his hazy directives to Laura, are common in Controllers. In addition, as we'll soon see, Laura knew that he was inclined to whine, blame, fall into gossip, and be vague about agreements—all attributes of Complainers. So as part of her preparation for the meeting with Cliff, she reviewed the best ways to approach Complainer and Controller bosses.

Laura's "big want" going into the meeting was to sell the team's proposal to her Controller-Complainer boss and obtain clear agreements on the next steps. To get ideas on how you might approach a similar boss, notice how she interweaves the tools presented earlier in this chapter with the Complainer- and Controller-specific tips in part II.

When she entered Cliff's office at 9:00 a.m., she found him pacing. "Boy, what a mess! We've worked with Highline longer than any other company. And now Peter's really mad at me. We go back a long way, you know. Laura, you gotta fix this or heads will roll."

Seeing Cliff caught in the whirlpool of his emotions, Laura stayed positive and relaxed as she reflected back to him. She knew that mirroring his agitated state—letting him know she understood his feelings—would strengthen her connection with him. "Peter has been one of our most long-standing clients, and we clearly see the importance of fixing the issues with Highline promptly and efficiently. I can understand that it's very frustrating to have your friend and such a large customer upset."

"You bet," he said.

"The good news is that the team has come together in a collaborative way to deal with the situation. We brainstormed for quite a while and considered several options, and after some healthy debate, we all agreed on one approach we think will make both you and Peter happy."

"I'm all ears, Laura. What did you come up with?"

She outlined the staged solution: She would continue to act as the overall project lead and liaison to Cliff, and Foster would run the operational side. She explained the roles of the individual team members, short-term staffing reassignments, and the intermediate milestone dates.

Cliff struggled to contain himself, finally blurting out, "But Peter will be all over me if we don't improve the performance immediately.

And if we eliminate Highline's maintenance fees, we'll never make our quarterly targets. You need to put Theresa's developers on the project. Call it "hazardous duty" or whatever you want, but—"

"Cliff," Laura gently interrupted, "it makes sense to me that you view performance improvements as important. I can understand your concern that forgoing Highline maintenance fees for a time might cause us to miss quarterly revenue targets. And you see shifting development resources as an alternative."

"Yeah, exactly. You nailed it."

"Thank you for bringing these issues up. Your concerns are legitimate, and we did consider them carefully in our discussions. We also kept coming back to the initial mandate: fix the Highline customer service and product issues, appease Peter, and maintain our own company's stability. I do want to make sure we're focusing on the right problem for you."

"Well, sure . . . but you also need to reassign some of Candace's people . . . and I'm not so sure it's a good idea to have Foster run the whole project. Maybe you should—"

Laura interrupted again, sensing that he was beginning to micromanage. "Yes, Cliff, and thank you for your concern. We did consider both reassigning Candace's staff and other operating leadership, as well as several other operational issues. Can I get your commitment to try our solution for a period of time before we make any directional changes?"

"I suppose . . . "

Laura continued, "As we move into implementation, I commit to keeping you abreast of any staffing reassignments, along with providing regular progress reports on the status of bug fixes, performance enhancements, and all new functionality. For now, I'd like your agreement on the roles of the four team members. I'd also like your approval of the proposed dates for the bug fixes, performance enhancements, new functionality, and the waiver on Highline's maintenance fees until all three of these commitments are achieved to Peter's satisfaction."

"Well, okay," Cliff said. "Just get all this done as soon as you can."

Seeing her boss's frustration with the project—and possibly with her—Laura was torn: Should she stop now with this vague agreement or push for his explicit approval of both the team roles and the intermediate dates? He still seemed agitated, and pressuring him further might prompt an emotional outburst, with her as the lightning rod. Nevertheless, she chose to get clarity.

"Cliff, I appreciate your support of our decision. We'll work as efficiently as possible on the resolution of the Highline problem. And to avoid any surprises, I would like to be clear on our roles and the intermediate milestones for the bug fixes, performance enhancements, and new functionality. Once again, here's what we propose."

She then re-explained the short-term staffing reassignments, Foster's specific role in running the operating side, and the checkpoint dates. "That's our plan," she said. "It's a stretch, but I feel confident. And I commit to approaching you any time I sense that the dates are in jeopardy or that the temporary staffing changes are having a negative impact on other parts of the business."

Then she went for the courageous close, looking him straight in the eyes. "Cliff, do I have your agreement on this plan?"

He paused, sighed, and said, "Okay, yes. I trust you to pull it off. Just keep me in the loop. I want to stay on top of this."

"Thank you for your confidence in us. I pledge to give you in-person or e-mail reports every other day and to let you know of any major changes immediately. Will that work for you?"

"Yeah, that'll work," he said. "But I have to tell you, Laura, I've still got some real concerns about Foster. He's in my office all the time pushing for more responsibility, and he's starting to drive me nuts. It sounds like you caved and let him run the Highline project. He just doesn't seem like a team player. What do you think?"

"Well, I can't comment on Foster outside of his interplay with our team. I can tell you that we've had some candid conversations, and the team and I now feel he can run the operating side of the project, reporting to me. I believe he appreciated the empowerment, and I also feel confident in my ability to manage him and hold him accountable."

Cliff sat back in his chair and sighed again. "I tell you, Laura, sometimes I wish I'd just stayed an independent consultant instead of starting Riva. I had a nice, comfortable life—no employees, managed my own time. And now, nothing but hassles. I bet you feel the same way sometimes, right?"

Laura sensed the no-win shift of the conversation. She respected Cliff's business development skills and appreciated the responsibility she had been given. She also decided to keep the relationship with him at a polite, transactional level so she wouldn't become entangled in his personal musings. She chose her words carefully, simply reflecting back his statements while remaining noncommittal.

"It sounds like you really liked your career as a consultant before founding Riva, just working by yourself and setting your own calendar. And I can see how hassles like the Highline situation could lead to reminiscing about the good parts of your old career. I can understand that. As for me, I'm just grateful to have the opportunity to work on projects I enjoy and hopefully make a difference in the company."

"Thank you, Laura. You're one of the best people I have here at Riva."

"Wow, Cliff—thanks. Your appreciation means a lot to me. I value your kind words and your support on this project. As I said, both the team and I are committed to a timely, cost-effective solution for Highline. I'll keep you informed on our progress and any changes in the plan. Unless there is something more you'd like to cover now, I'd like to get back to the Highline team. We have a lot to do."

Epilogue

In the early stages of the meeting, when Cliff was consumed by his drama, Laura built relational capital with him by remaining calm and unattached. She thoughtfully reflected back his emotions and reframed his ramblings to show her understanding of them. Most bosses like to receive good news, so she focused on the positive outcomes of the team meeting. She kindly, yet firmly, held her ground when he slipped into both his Controller persona (threats, micromanaging, and vague agreements) and Complainer persona (whining and seeking a confidant). Laura sidestepped or deflected these antics.

She used both Controller-specific antidotes (clear agreements, matching his power, praising delegation) and Complainer-specific antidotes (honoring his ideas, fully supporting him, avoiding a personal relationship). When he went off on tangents, she kept bringing him back to the "big wants" to get his approval for the team's proposal and his agreement on next steps.

It was rare for Cliff to offer appreciation, acknowledging Laura as one of the best people in the company. It might be tempting to deflect or diminish this appreciation from a superior ("Oh, it was nothing"), but Laura appropriately received it, accepting this "gift" from Cliff. In so doing, she further strengthened her relationship with her boss.

BEING AN AUTHENTIC LEADER

Our goal in this book has been to inspire you toward a drama-free office—a productive and fun work environment where interpersonal issues are faced swiftly, problems are addressed collaboratively, individuals are appreciated, and successes are celebrated.

A drama-free office is made up of drama-free individuals—starting with you. When you choose—and it's always a choice—to show up with curiosity, candor, courage, and appreciation, you encourage your coworkers to do the same. You become the inspiration for your boss, your partner, your cofounder, or a team member to catch the "authenticity bug." Drama-free individuals forge nonjudgmental, drama-free relationships—the cornerstones of the drama-free office.

Individuals in drama-free relationships support one another in keeping agreements and hold one another accountable for commitments. They practice the disciplines outlined in this book to sustain clean, authentic interactions. They help each other avoid the dramatic behaviors (blaming, gossip, stonewalling, cynicism, resentment, enabling) that threaten to cripple almost every office. And when a colleague falters and falls into drama, they initiate the direct conversation that restores authentic connection and energy-enhancing collaboration.

Over time, others will observe how you and your authenticity allies model drama-free relationships. Some—hopefully most—will begin to shift out of their patterns of complaining, cynicism, controlling, and caretaking. Authenticity breeds authenticity.

But not always.

Regardless of how you behave, some of your associates, and perhaps your boss, might choose—again, it's their choice, even if unconscious or unacknowledged—the false security and comfort of their dramatic behaviors. Authenticity carries the risk of vulnerability, betrayal, and embarrassment, and they might prefer the structure, sterility, and safety of a dramatic or transactional relationship.

Acknowledge and accept their choice while staying authentic with yourself and in your core relationships. Strive to remain understanding and compassionate toward your drama-prone colleagues without feeling obligated to rescue them. Accept, perhaps with sadness, the transactional nature of the relationship, and then manage their behavior. Many times, we have seen drama-laden people experience an authenticity epiphany simply by observing—and inwardly envying—the drama-free behaviors of their coworkers.

So, stay on course and commit to authenticity. You might never know the timing and extent of your impact on others. One of the best ways to sustain authenticity in your life is to adopt the mantras shown on page 184. They are the guideposts of a mature professional. Repeat them as often as necessary until they become second nature. Do this, and you will become the authentic professional your organization and the world needs.

MANTRAS OF AUTHENTIC PROFESSIONALS	
Adopt these mantras as the foundation of your own authenticity.	
DRAMA TYPE	**AUTHENTICITY MANTRAS**
COMPLAINER	• I am grounded and disciplined.
	• I am strong and resilient.
	• I get the job done.
CYNIC	• I am an enthusiastic motivator.
	• I appreciate others' gifts and perspectives.
	• I am fully engaged.
CONTROLLER	• I am patient with others and myself.
	• I embrace others' beliefs and ideas.
	• I take myself lightly.
CARETAKER	• I trust others to take care of themselves.
	• I nurture myself.
	• I am direct, decisive, and empowering.
ALL DRAMA TYPES	• I take full responsibility for whatever is happening in my life.
	• I relate to others with candor and compassion.
	• I embrace curiosity as the springboard for learning and personal growth.
	• I choose collaboration to set the stage for synergy and creative solutions.

MATURE RESPONSES TO DRAMATIC PEOPLE

The following table presents the various dramatic personas often encountered in the workplace. Even with the best intentions to be drama-free, it's easy to get triggered by their behaviors and fall into an emotion-driven reaction. Instead, choose the mature response shown in the table.

HOW TO SHIFT OUT OF YOUR OWN DRAMA
WHEN WORKING WITH DRAMATIC PEOPLE

	THE OTHER PERSON'S BEHAVIOR	THE EMOTION-DRIVEN REACTION	THE MATURE RESPONSE
The Perfectionist	• Opinionated • Impatient • Rigid • Obsessive • Judgmental • Blunt	• Placate ("Whatever you want . . .") • Set them up to fail or look stupid • Engage in heated debate	• Acknowledge to yourself their intention for things to be done efficiently and thoroughly • Be accurate and detailed in your own work • Maintain a positive tone • Use Controller tips
The Worrywart	• People-pleasing • Clingy • Indecisive	• Force into taking action • Dismiss as a loser • Become their therapist	• Acknowledge to yourself their need to feel liked • Focus on positives • Offer options and applaud decisiveness • Use Caretaker and Complainer tips
The Center of Attention	• Self-promoting • Boastful • Grandiose • Bombastic • Flamboyant	• Set them up to fail or look stupid • Mock or gossip behind their back • Ignore them • Fawn over them	• Acknowledge to yourself their need to be appreciated • Be kind, yet direct • Praise their patience and empowerment of others • Use Controller and Complainer tips

THE OTHER PERSON'S BEHAVIOR	THE EMOTION-DRIVEN REACTION	THE MATURE RESPONSE
The Truth Twister • Manipulative • Rationalizing • Deflecting • Secretive	• Ignore your own warning signals and acquiesce • Engage in heated debate • Accuse them of lying	• Acknowledge to yourself their desire to create a great end, regardless of the means • Focus on unarguable facts • Set up and monitor clear metrics • Use Cynic and Controller tips
The Misunderstood Genius • Moody • Self-righteous • Self-absorbed • Temperamental • Pretentious	• Set them up to fail or look stupid • Mock or gossip behind their back • Attack or belittle them in public • Hide out from them • Fawn over their brilliance	• Acknowledge to yourself their need to be appreciated and understood • Invite their insights • Praise them for seeking feedback • Use Complainer, Cynic, and Controller tips
The Watchdog • Doubtful • Suspicious • Hypervigilant • Reactive • Pessimistic • Fearful • Distrusting	• Ignore or belittle their concerns • Publicly chastise them • Get caught up in their fears	• Acknowledge to yourself their need to protect and feel safe • Help them see positive outcomes instead of potential catastrophes • Use Complainer, Cynic, and Caretaker tips

continues on next page

THE OTHER PERSON'S BEHAVIOR	THE EMOTION-DRIVEN REACTION	THE MATURE RESPONSE
The Rebel or Contrarian • Defiant • Confrontational • Forceful • Willful • Angry • Disdainful of authority	• Avoid them or get out of their way • Try to muzzle them • Attack them • Commiserate with them	• Acknowledge to yourself their desire for "a better world" • Be direct, truthful, and fair, while holding your ground • Let them get a "win" • Use Complainer, Cynic, and Controller tips
The Space Case • Complacent • Agreeable • Nonconfrontational • Oblivious	• Belittle them • Hammer them into action • Ignore them as too "out there"	• Acknowledge to yourself their need for connection and camaraderie • Focus on one thing at a time • Set up and monitor clear metrics • Use Complainer and Caretaker tips
The Uninvited Advisor • Relentless • Smothering • Oblivious to receptivity of others	• Admonish them ("Get away from me!") • Ignore them • Placate them ("Whatever you say . . .") • Belittle them ("Thanks, Dad")	• Acknowledge to yourself their need to be helpful and feel appreciated • Genuinely listen and reflect . . . to a point • Politely, but firmly, set your boundaries (timelines, extent of advice you are willing to receive) • Use Controller and Caretaker tips

	THE OTHER PERSON'S BEHAVIOR	THE EMOTION-DRIVEN REACTION	THE MATURE RESPONSE
The Rabbit Chaser	• Frequently on a tangent • Unable to focus • Prone to hijack agendas • Self-centered	• Acquiesce; let them hijack the agenda • Debate irrelevant topics with them • Publicly chastise them	• Acknowledge to yourself their need to explore various options • Set clear discussion boundaries • Channel their attention to detail toward bigger-picture issues • Use Complainer, Cynic, and Controller tips
The Constant Apologizer	• Always willing to admit fault (even if it's not theirs) • Fearful of making a mistake • Self-deprecating • Over-attentive to detail	• Dismiss them as weak or a loser • Reduce their responsibilities with no explanation • Ignore or tolerate them • Place them in a silo	• Acknowledge to yourself their need to be liked • Honor their emotion and immediately follow with a genuine appreciation of them • Model lightheartedness • Use Caretaker tips
The Ultimate Pessimist	• Argumentative • Suspicious • Blaming • Stubborn	• Strangle them • Run and hide from them • Agree with them, hoping they'll eventually stop	• Acknowledge to yourself their need to have a voice • Solicit their ideas and recommendations • Invite them to focus on what they control

continues on next page

THE OTHER PERSON'S BEHAVIOR	THE EMOTION-DRIVEN REACTION	THE MATURE RESPONSE
The Martyr • Noble resignation ("If I don't do it no one else will.") • Fatalistic ("I must suffer for the cause.") • Indispensible ("You need me.")	• Ignore them • Belittle them • Pity them • Commiserate with them • Rescue them	• Acknowledge to yourself their need to be seen and appreciated • Help them clarify what they really want for themselves—that doesn't require suffering for "the cause" • Model upbeat behavior • Use Complainer and Caretaker tips
The Bitter Soldier • Demeaning • Shaming • Morally superior • Passive-aggressive • Volatile	• Isolate and Ignore them • Run and hide from them • Counterattack them • Take their remarks personally	• Acknowledge to yourself their inconsistent behavior; it's not about you • Use ultimatums to get behaviors you require from them • Isolate and closely manage them • Praise positive behaviors and consistency • Anticipate rebellion • Use Cynic and Caretaker tips

THE OTHER PERSON'S BEHAVIOR	THE EMOTION-DRIVEN REACTION*	THE MATURE RESPONSE
The Benevolent Autocrat (as the boss) • Overbearing protector • Micromanager • Narcissistic ("I'm special. You need to trust me because I know what's best.") • Noble savior	• Question them (and risk triggering their wrath) • Become their servant (to avoid their wrath) • Fawn over them • Challenge them (at your own peril) • Mock them behind their backs • Whine to your peers • Enlist your peers in a mutiny • Fear their inconsistencies • Numbly resign ("The situation is hopeless.")	• Acknowledge to yourself their need to be seen and appreciated • Calmly and politely ask for complete instructions and clear agreements • Appreciate them for delegating and empowering • Appreciate them for soliciting your input • Use tips for managing Controller and Caretaker bosses
The Weak King (as the boss) • Impulsive • Can't grasp subtleties or nuances • Insecure; easily threatened • Indecisive or panicky under pressure • Pompous ("I'm special because I'm the boss.")		• Acknowledge to yourself their desperate need to be seen and valued • Maintain a civil, transactional relationship while staying below their radar screen • Use tips for managing Controller and Complainer bosses

continues on next page

* *The emotion-driven reactions to The Benevolent Autocrat, The Weak King, and The Cunning Dictator bosses are similar.*

THE OTHER PERSON'S BEHAVIOR	THE EMOTION-DRIVEN REACTION	THE MATURE RESPONSE
The Cunning Dictator (as the boss) • Unpredictable • Wrathful • Devious • Loathes weakness • Combative • Punitive	• Question them (and risk triggering their wrath) • Become their servant (to avoid their wrath) • Fawn over them • Challenge them (at your own peril) • Mock them behind their backs • Whine to your peers • Enlist your peers in a mutiny • Fear their inconsistencies • Numbly resign ("The situation is hopeless.")	• Acknowledge to yourself their obsession for power and control • Maintain a civil, transactional relationship while staying below their radar screen • Stay calm, polite, or even deferential in all interactions • Reflect back their emotional displays without getting triggered • Use tips for managing Controller and Cynic bosses
All Types • Usually (but not always) unaware of the impact of their behavior • Innately drawn to being "right"	• Attack them • Avoid them • Acquiesce to them • Debate them • Dismiss them	• Acknowledge to yourself the noble intention or desire behind their behavior • Use a blend of the Complainer, Cynic, Controller, and Caretaker tips

THE DRAMA
SELF-ASSESSMENT

If you're serious about displaying authenticity in the workplace, take the following Drama Self-Assessment. For each drama-based behavior shown in the table, place a check mark in the column that reflects the frequency with which this behavior shows up in your life. Then, invite two or more of your work associates to evaluate you. Compare their assessments with how you see yourself. An expanded online version of this assessment that allows for others to evaluate you may be found at **www.DramaFreeOffice.com**.

Scoring: Each **Never or Rarely** counts as zero; each **Occasionally**

DRAMA SELF-ASSESSMENT

	Dramatic behavior	Never or Rarely	Occa-sionally	Often
1	You have a strong urge to tell others why they are wrong and you are right.			
2	When things go wrong, you blame someone or something outside of your control, or rationalize your inability to take action.			
3	You tend to show polite interest outwardly while inwardly clinging to your point of view.			
4	You feel misunderstood and unappreciated.			
5	You find fault with the way others present their views.			
6	You display anger, irritation, or resentment in a nonverbal way.			
7	You commit to doing tasks without the time or resources to actually get them done.			
8	You commit to doing something when you have no real intention of actually doing it.			
9	You complain to others about people or decisions.			
10	You ask a lot of "why" questions, probing others' intentions.			
11	You interrupt others and then interject a different perspective.			
12	You interpret others' viewpoints as an attack and prepare your retaliation.			
13	You express your disagreement with anger or annoyance.			
14	You either actively seek or inwardly yearn for the recognition of others.			
15	You regularly check an internal scoreboard, assessing how you measure up against others.			
16	You often say to yourself, "I deserve [something good]."			
17	You often say to yourself, "I don't deserve [something bad]."			
18	You quickly acquiesce to others' views in the face of conflict or disagreement.			
19	You struggle to acknowledge and experience your own emotions.			
20	You struggle to acknowledge and honor emotions in others.			
21	You are quick to point out the downside of an issue or topic.			
	Totals			

counts as 1; each **Often** counts as 3. Compute the total. A total of less than 12 indicates reasonably mature behavior. If both your self-assessment and others' assessment of you is in this range, you're likely capable of guiding others into more authentic behaviors. A total that's between 13 and 20 indicates some sabotaging behaviors that will hamper authenticity in your relationships. A total greater than 20 indicates a high likelihood of ongoing drama-based behavior.

ONLINE TOOLS FOR ASSESSING THE AUTHENTICITY OF YOUR OFFICE

The authors have developed a suite of online assessments designed to evaluate the levels of authenticity—and levels of drama—of individuals in several workplace environments, including:

- Executive teams
- Partnerships
- Family businesses
- Work groups or project teams
- Other small groups (e.g., Young Presidents' Organization forums and other accountability groups)

These online assessments offer an optional 360 component (i.e., evaluations of a single individual by multiple coworkers, such as subordinates, peers, or superiors in the organization). They are an ideal complement to an organization's annual review process.

Each assessment yields a customized summary report outlining the areas where an individual needs to grow or change to reduce drama and enhance collaboration in his or her interactions.

For more information on Online Authenticity Assessments, go to **www.DramaFreeOffice.com**.

ACKNOWLEDGMENTS

Many authenticity seekers assisted us in preparing *The Drama-Free Office*. We are grateful to:

Our "Inspiration Team," who encouraged us during the conception and editing of this book: Judy Wells Warner, Nate Klemp, Dave Bloom, and Jim Kochalka.

The illustration and editing team, who transformed a raw manuscript into flowing prose and compelling pictures: Kayla Morelli, Marco Morelli, Sandra Jonas, and the professionals at Greenleaf Book Group (Bill Crawford, Aaron Hierholzer, Neil Gonzalez, Katelynn Knudson, Bryan Carroll, and Clint Greenleaf).

Our reviewers, all committed to living drama-free lives, who challenged us and encouraged us to challenge and encourage others:

Andy Putterman	Bruce Smith	Diana Chapman
Steve Barnes	Steve Lockshin	Ron Boehm
Chris Haase	Michael Bloch	Stephen Liptrap
Dick Simon	Scott Lynn	David Stoup
Dick Schulte	Mark Wiseman	Frank Buonanotte
Kent McClelland	David Barlow	Stephen Green
Mark Tribus	Pat Christen	Larry Miles
Peter Durhager	Jim Barnett	Peter Evans
Dave Phillips	Michael Brown	Jim Dethmer
Scott Gould	Beat Steiner	Devin Schain

We would also like to acknowledge the Forum for Consciousness and Leadership, whose members are committed to leading Drama-Free Organizations.

The tools presented in part IV of this book draw from the collective wisdom of the following authors.

Gay and Kathlyn Hendricks lead an International Learning Center that teaches core skills for conscious living. Their groundbreaking work over the past three decades has guided people to more authentic relationships and whole-person learning. For more information, go to www.hendricks.com.

Kate Ludeman and Eddie Erlandson's excellent book *Radical Change, Radical Results* offers valuable insights on accountability, candor, appreciation, and making clear agreements. For more information, go to www.worthethic.com.

Don Riso and Russ Hudson are two of the foremost teachers on awareness and presence. Their work centers on the Enneagram personality typing system. Their signature book *The Wisdom of the Enneagram* provides a comprehensive, easy-to-understand explanation of this profound model of human interactions. For more information, go to www.enneagraminstitute.com.

Tommy Spaulding is an inspirational speaker and author on relationship authenticity. His bestseller *It's Not Just Who You Know* presents valuable tips for maximizing your ROR (return on relationships). For more information, go to www.tommyspaulding.com.

ABOUT THE AUTHORS

Jim Warner and **Kaley Klemp** are devoted to guiding organizations, family businesses, and professional partnerships on how to expand their leadership skills while fostering enduring authenticity and collaboration within their teams. Whether for entire corporations, executive teams, small groups, couples, or individuals, Jim and Kaley are experts in creating collaborative, productive interactions. Their research for *The Drama-Free Office* is based on their work with over 2,500 CEOs and their executive teams worldwide.

Jim Warner is an entrepreneur and transitions expert. During the 1980s and early 1990s, he founded, grew, ran, and eventually sold an international software company. After a three-year "midlife sabbatical," he formed OnCourse International as the platform for guiding both businesses in transition and individuals seeking personal transformation.

Jim's Business Transition work is a blend of CEO advisory services, authenticity diagnostics, executive team development, and succession planning. The overarching goal in all engagements is productive, efficient, drama-free interactions among managers and leaders at all levels of the organization.

Jim's Personal Transformation work with individuals, couples, and family units includes whole-life assessments, life-planning retreats, ongoing coaching, and life-enhancement programs. All offerings help committed clients to find a deeper sense of life meaning, to forge and sustain authentic relationships, and to live out their innate essence.

Jim is the author of *Facing Pain—Embracing Love: The Map to Authentic Living* and *Aspirations of Greatness: Mapping the Midlife Leader's Reconnection to Self and Soul,* as well as the audio series *When Having It All Isn't Enough.*

Jim and Judy Wells Warner have been married for thirty-five years and live in Boulder, Colorado. Jim is an alumnus of the University of Michigan and Harvard Business School (OPM program). He is a member of World Presidents' Organization.

Visit Jim's website at **www.JimWarnerGroup.com**.

Kaley Klemp is a sought-after facilitator, speaker, and executive coach. She is an expert in small-group dynamics and leadership development. Kaley helps strengthen communication and conflict resolution skills as keys to improve performance. Since 2004, she has worked with executives and their teams to uncover and address the issues that block peak performance. Kaley helps teams build trust, develop authentic relationships, and use creative collaboration to foster a common vision, develop a strategic plan, and achieve superior results. Teams that work with Kaley appreciate her interactive style and her ability to translate theory into enduring practices.

A favorite with Young Presidents' Organization (YPO) forums and chapters, Kaley has facilitated retreats for more than 175 member and spouse forums throughout the world. She has helped executive teams of some of the world's most prominent companies create cultures of responsibility and appreciation. She is the author of *13 Guidelines for Effective Teams*.

Kaley is a graduate of Stanford University, where she earned a B.A. in International Relations and an M.A. in Sociology, with a focus on Organizational Behavior. She is an avid athlete, spending time practicing yoga, skiing, hiking, and mountain biking. She lives in Los Angeles, California, with her husband Nate.

Visit Kaley's website at **www.KaleyKlemp.com**.

Jim and Kaley are inspiring speakers and change agents. Both individually and as a high-energy team, they have delivered hundreds of keynote addresses, team-building retreats, and experiential workshops to companies, associations, and non-profits designed to engage, entertain, and inspire high achievers. Every event is customized to optimize the immediate take-home value for the target audience (CEOs, professionals, managers, couples, work teams, or leaders in transition).

To engage Kaley, Jim, or both for your next meeting or event, please visit their website at **www.DramaFreeOffice.com** or call +1 303-449-7770.

18055304R00127

Printed in Great Britain
by Amazon